1857 A FRIEND IN NEED
1887 FRIENDSHIP FORGOTTEN

1857 A FRIEND IN NEED
1887 FRIENDSHIP FORGOTTEN

AN EPISODE IN INDIAN FOREIGN OFFICE ADMINISTRATION

WILLIAM DIGBY

"I had the satisfaction of offering to the Maharaja Jung Bahadur, in full Durbar, my cordial thanks for the aid which the Government of India had received from him and from his brave soldiers, and *my assurance that the friendly conduct of his Government and the exertions and successes of his troops*, WOULD BE HELD IN GRATEFUL RECOLLECTION, NOT LESS IN ENGLAND THAN IN INDIA'-

LORD CANNING, May 30, 1858

'Of one thing you may be sure, THE BRITISH GOVERNMENT....DOES NOT FORGET *those, who have deserved well at its hands'*-

LORD LANSDOWNE at Quetta, Oct, 1889.

GYAN

Published by

GYAN

Gyan Publishing House
5, Ansari Road
Daryaganj, New Delhi-110002
Phone: 011-47034999, 9811692060
E-mail: books@gyanbooks.com

Distribution Network
gyanbooks.com
India, USA, Canada, UK, Australia, France

ISBN : 978-81-212-3409-2 (PB)
First Published, London, 1890

2nd Impression 2020

Printed at: Gyan Press, Delhi.

1857 A Friend in Need
1887 Friendship Forgotten
Author: William Digby

1857. A FRIEND IN NEED.

1887. FRIENDSHIP FORGOTTEN.

AN EPISODE IN INDIAN FOREIGN OFFICE ADMINISTRATION.

BY

WILLIAM DIGBY, C.I.E.

'I had the satisfaction of offering to the Maharajah Jung Bahadur, in full Durbar, my cordial thanks for the aid which the Government of India had received from him and from his brave soldiers, and *my assurance that the friendly conduct of his Government and the exertions and successes of his troops*, WOULD BE HELD IN GRATEFUL RECOLLECTION, NOT LESS IN ENGLAND THAN IN INDIA.'—LORD CANNING, May 30, 1858.

'Of one thing you may be sure, THE BRITISH GOVERNMENT . . . . DOES NOT FORGET *those who have deserved well at its hands*.'—LORD LANSDOWNE at Quetta, Oct., 1889.

London:

INDIAN POLITICAL AGENCY, 25, CRAVEN STREET, CHARING CROSS.

1890.

'I KNOW MY NATION IS NOT EQUAL TO YOURS, NOR OUR POWER TO YOURS. BUT THERE IS ONE THING IN WHICH WE ARE AND OUGHT EVER TO BE EQUAL, NAMELY, *JUSTICE—MUTUAL JUSTICE*.'—SIR JUNG BAHADUR.

Two years in recent British Indian history. Two incidents affording a striking contrast.

In 1857

Sir Jung Bahadur places the resources of the Kingdom of Nepal at the service of the Governor-General of India. The offer is accepted. Less than a year after Lord Canning expresses cordial thanks for the aid which the Prime Minister of Nepal and his brave soldiers rendered in the suppression of the Mutiny, and adds: 'The friendly conduct of his Government, and the exertions and successes of his troops, will be held in grateful recollection not less in England than in India.' That Lord Canning was speaking the mind of England in so saying the English newspapers of the day bear testimony.

In 1886 and 1887

another Viceroy and Governor-General of India is, in view of what was said in 1858, asked to interest himself in Nepal, and to show some kindness to the family of India's friend in Mutiny days. The Dowager Queen of Nepal, a daughter of Sir Jung Bahadur, and other relatives of the late Prime Minister of Nepal, are refugees in India. They have been driven from their country and their homes by an act of wholly unjustifiable usurpation, the country not being misgoverned, and by a series of peculiarly base assassinations of most dearly beloved relatives. The Marquis of Dufferin and Ava is Viceroy and Governor-General. In culture, in broad-mindedness, and in a chivalrous sensitiveness to every honourable obligation binding upon the British nation Lord Dufferin is regarded as without a superior, and as not having many equals. Nevertheless, incredible as it may seem, with Lord Canning's plighted word on behalf of both England and India brought specially to his attention, his Excellency leaves the distressed daughter and nephew of Sir Jung Bahadur wholly without sympathy, and refrains from exercising that friendly intervention which was asked for and which could so easily have been rendered. One explanation, apparently, is alone possible. The Indian Foreign Office evidently had no copy of Lord Canning's letter to the Secret Committee of the East India Company, and Sir Mortimer Durand was, therefore, unable to verify the accuracy of the statements attributed to the Viceroy of thirty years ago. Even the Foreign Office at Calcutta could not, otherwise, have advised his Excellency to imitate Lord Nelson and turn a blind eye to the words quoted, and to act a churlish and ungrateful part by remaining deaf to the appeals again and again made to him. Nor, once more, but for some occult or pedantic reason could the actions of the ex-King Theebaw of Burma have eclipsed the fame of Sir Jung Bahadur of Nepal, and have driven all thoughts of the latter's deserts from the viceregal mind. Generally, Lord Dufferin is capable of taking note of more than one thing at a time.

Further, in 1886, the Marchioness of Dufferin and Ava—a lady who has proved herself to be the worthy companion in culture, sympathy, and chivalry of her husband—is, permission for the visit having been given by the political authorities, visited by the distressed Dowager Queen of Nepal. Strange to relate, her Excellency is not moved by the woes of her illustrious visitor, nor does she in any way realise why this lady should go to the Viceroy's wife with high hopes. It cannot be Lady Dufferin is influenced by that shallowness of thought which considers that, under a skin of a colour different from one's own, human nature changes and becomes other than that of which one is conscious in regard to one's self and one's race-fellows. To not a few English people in India it is oftentimes necessary to say: 'Hath not an Indian eyes? Hath not an Indian hands, organs, dimensions, senses, affections, passions? Fed with the same food, hurt with the same weapons, subject to the same diseases, healed by the same means, warmed and cooled by the same winter and summer as a European is?' Lady Dufferin never needed to ask this question. Indian womanhood appealed to her the moment almost that she landed at Bombay, certainly before she had long been in residence at Calcutta. Throughout the period of her husband's rule she never wearied in her endeavours to promote, in the broadest sense, the welfare of the women of India. She has left in the East an imperishable record of her kindliness and generous nature and unflagging goodwill; and, scattered throughout India, are many institutions for the amelioration of suffering which owe their existence to the spirit of goodness her exertions and example called forth. It is the barest justice to Lady Dufferin to say this. And, having said it, the wonder grows that the Dowager Queen of Nepal should have visited Government House, have conversed with the Vice-reine, and have told her troubles, and yet have failed to evoke any emotion in Lady Dufferin's heart. Her Excellency has given to the world her account of the interview. That account will be found, extracted from the first volume of 'Our Viceregal Life in India', on pp. 103-106 of this record. The passages cited have been read by many in India and by some in England with mingled feelings of surprise and sadness. Little need be said about them: respect for her ladyship requires that little should be said. Justice, however, demands that some mention should be made. The cynical contempt for all the past events in India which require friendly consideration for anyone of Asiatic parentage must indeed be colossal when its effect upon Lady Dufferin — all unknown and unsuspected by her ladyship it must be believed — was so marked. The grievances suffered by individuals in consequence of the prevalence of this contempt for, and ignorance of, the past incidents of administration, and of personages with whom we have had dealings, serious and calamitous as they are, are as nothing compared with the grave peril to the State which is involved in such a state of things.

The 'grateful recollection not less in England than in India' vouchsafed with sincerity to Sir Jung Bahadur by Lord Canning has been wholly effaced from the minds of the rulers of India. There remains England, whose 'grateful recollection' Lord Canning felt himself justified in proffering. It is the object of this little work to ascertain whether gratitude for such unique and most valuable aid as Sir Jung Bahadur rendered is as little cherished in England as, apparently, it is in India. The Dowager Queen of Nepal, her cousin General Dhoje Nursing, and other Nepalese refugees in India, entertain no doubt on this point. They believe British statesmen who ruled India in past days said what they meant and meant what they said, and that the British nation will stand by what they said. Not statesmen only have spoken. H.R.H. the Prince of Wales, and not a few of the nobles of England, have been lavish in their acknowledgments of Nepalese help and goodwill to Britain in India, and, it must be presumed, have not been unmindful of the obligations consequential on such acknowledgments. The belief is cherished, with a confidence and fidelity that have in them much that is touching, that services so splendid and so timely as those rendered by Sir Jung Bahadur in 1857 and in 1858, and the subsequent hearty recognition of those services, cannot fail to bear some fruit. The crop looked for is not large. Only a little thoughtful consideration, and friendly intervention in a quarter where one word spoken with firmness from the Viceroy and Governor-General of India would be sufficient, in redemption alike of Treaty provisions and personal promises, are sought. These pages will have been written in vain if at least this much of justice is not granted through the friendly efforts of English people, or, better still, of his own generous and grateful motion, by the Marquess of Lansdowne, Viceroy and Governor-General of India, with whom is the power and, I would fain hope, the will also to do all that is desired and all that is due.

25, Craven Street, Charing Cross, London:
January, 1890.

TABLE OF CONTENTS.

INTRODUCTION.

CHAPTER I.

THE KINGDOM OF NEPAL.

CHAPTER IV.

SHAKSPERE'S 'MACBETH' IN NEPALESE ROYAL AND NOBLE LIFE.

CHAPTER V.

A NEPHEW'S GRATITUDE, AND HIS MANNER OF SHOWING IT.

CHAPTER VI.

A DOWAGER QUEEN: HER TREATMENT IN CALCUTTA.

CHAPTER VII.

A NEPALESE NOBLE'S FORTUNE.

APPENDIX.

I.

II.

ILLUSTRATIONS.

The story told in the following pages is one with which, unfortunately, the annals of our Indian Empire are familiar. No public department in any country, despotically or constitutionally ruled, ever had so short a memory, or one more oblivious to the teachings of history and the claims of justice, than the Calcutta Foreign Office has proved itself to possess. Its course is strewn with wrecks. No greater danger to all that is stable in our Eastern territory than is involved in this circumstance, can be imagined. In the interests of the Empire the policy followed by Indian Foreign Secretaries is strongly to be deprecated.

The incidents set forth at some length in the pages of this little work, relate to a State in friendly alliance with us. The reigning family, and the connections of an ex-Prime Minister, in whose family the office was hereditary, have special claims, the strongest claims of which the comity of nations permits, to our consideration for services rendered to us in the past—rendered, too, at a time when friendly assistance was of special value and of supreme importance. In saying this everything should be considered as said. That any persons have a claim on the Government of India for help freely given should, in itself, be an assurance that the claim will be favourably considered, and, if found to be fair, be immediately conceded. This is the spirit in which Lord Lansdowne evidently desires to rule. Speaking at a Durbar held at Quetta in the third week of October, 1889, his Excellency said: 'Of one thing you may be sure, the British Government . . . . does not forget those who have deserved well at its hands.' If this noble utterance were indeed acted upon, this work would not have been written. There would have been no need for it.

The government of the State in question is subverted by an ambitious officer; its Prime Minister, a tried friend of the British Government, is foully murdered; many of its Princes and chief nobles are either massacred, forced into exile, or thrown into captivity; its King, a boy of some twelve summers, is virtually made a prisoner in his own palace. In these circumstances the senior member of the Royal family of this unhappy State and the exiled Princes appeal to the ex-Viceroy of India for help; their appeal is rejected with what seems like studied contempt: what, indeed, *is* studied contempt, as documents to be quoted hereafter will show; and the world witnesses the strange spectacle of a Christian Government flinging aside all treaty and moral obligations, and allying itself with murderers and rebels. Such an alliance, reprehensible at all times, must be doubly so where it leads, as it has done in this case, to the oppression of an entire people.

Not many months have passed since England withdrew her ambassador from Paris so that he might not take a part in the celebration of a Festival of Peace, because that festival was associated with the French Revolution of 1789; but in India the pious horror of revolutions which the Government of England cherish is singularly manifested by their warmly supporting traitors and murderers who sought, not national emancipation, but power and rule for themselves, by a peculiarly cold-blooded and brutal murder, and at the sacrifice of their country's independence. The *Pioneer*, of Allahabad, spoke with grave wisdom when it declared that the recognition of the new administration in Nepal was 'a repulsive alternative with a discouraging moral to it'. The 'repulsive alternative' and 'discouraging moral' lay in a Viceroy of India 'recognising a ruler who seizes the sceptre red-handed'. It is difficult to conceive a Government to whom such a course should be more repugnant than to the Government of India. Nevertheless, the 'repulsive alternative' was accepted, and the 'discouraging moral' condoned.

The apologists of the Indian Foreign Office, in defence of its strange policy—a policy so full of ingratitude and so fruitful of mischief—in reference to Nepal, say, 'The Durbar having appointed Bir Shumshere to be the Prime Minister, our Government had no other course but to recognise him'. This is an utterly false plea. The Durbar exists only in the imagination of our political officers. Having called it into existence, the conscience of Sir Mortimer Durand,[1] in this instance most scrupulous, will not suffer him to interfere in the affairs of a neighbouring State; and he has, therefore, placed his own brother in charge of the Residency at Khatmandu, in order to maintain his policy of non-interference intact! It is further

[1] Foreign Secretary to the Government of India.

alleged, as a reason why the Indian Government should take no action, that China is Nepal's suzerain, and we are bound to respect China's rights. Unfortunately for this contention, facts are against it. The Government of India went to war with Nepal in 1814, without for a moment thinking of China's suzerainty; nor did China help her feudatory in that conflict, or take any steps to prevent the cession of Nepalese territory to India.

In our treaties and relations with Nepal, the paramountcy of China is ignored; the setting-up of this plea is evidently an afterthought. It is, without doubt, a wise principle strictly to abstain from interference in the internal affairs of Indian States; but have the Indian Government in the past, rigidly observed it in their dealings with them? Prompted by earth-hunger, or some equally depraved form of appetite, they have, on the contrary, constantly interfered in their internal administration, until State after State has been absorbed in British dominions, and is now coloured on maps with the Imperial red. As regards Nepal itself, on divers occasions the Indian Government concerned themselves with its affairs, sometimes in a friendly, at others in a hostile, spirit. Colonel Kirkpatrick's mission to Khatmandu in 1793, to mediate between China and Nepal, on the outbreak of hostilities between these powers; their interposition in securing a suitable provision for Ran Bahadur Shah, an ex-King of Nepal; their action in 1839 in procuring the dismissal of a Nepalese Ministry, believed to be adverse to the British alliance; and their detention of Matahar Sing—a Nepalese Sirdar, and, subsequently, Prime Minister of Nepal—as a State prisoner for many years; all these, it is clear, furnish abundant proofs of British intervention in the past, both in assertion of our rights, and by way of a practical expression of our amity to our ally. These precedents leave the Indian authorities entirely without excuse in the course of conduct they have seen fit to adopt towards those whose story will be told in these pages, and to whom they were bound, by ties of commonest gratitude, to show great consideration, and for whom they should have been ready to take much trouble.

Another reason given for the too hasty recognition and support of Bir Shumshere, whose act of high-handed and murderous violence will be found fully detailed, is his alleged popularity among his countrymen. This is no more true than was the boasted popularity of British rule in Upper Burmah when dacoit bands were resisting British arms in every district. The people of Nepal are quiet, solely for want of arms and of leaders; but to infer from this seeming tranquillity their cordial acceptance of Bir Shumshere's rule, would be as rational as to conclude that a volcano is extinct because for a time its fires are quiet and its action is not perceptible to the distant observer, who knows nothing of the unseen workings destined speedily to blaze forth. The suddenness of the *coup d'état* at Khatmandu in 1885, and the unexpected British support of the usurper, at first stunned the Nepalese.

> ''Twas listening fear and dumb amazement all!'

They now keenly feel his ruthless mode of rule, and the

whole country is seething with discontent. The insurrection of 1887, though identified with Ranbir Jung, one of the refugees, was only a popular movement; it failed because it was premature and the organisers too precipitate in their action.[1] But that Bir Shumshere's fate is sealed is, in the opinion of observers whose views are entitled to much respect, abundantly clear. That such a consummation is, from England's point of view in India, strongly to be desired, the well-informed writer in the *St. James's Gazette* (quoted below) makes

---

[1] THE INSURRECTION IN NEPAL.

(*St. James's Gazette*, Dec., 1887.)

A revolution in Nepal has been expected for some time past. There was an abortive attempt at a rising in June. Emissaries from Ranbir Jung, a son of the once famous Jung Bahadur (the Talleyrand from the Himalayas, whose diamonds were so much admired in London nearly forty years ago), had been inciting the soldiers to mutiny, and two serious outbreaks took place. Ranbir Jung, till the other day, was living in uneasy exile at Benares, along with General Jeet Jung, formerly Commander-in-Chief in Nepal. Another Nepalese exile living there is the Jetha Maharani, mother of the titular 'King of the Gurkhas', as the Maharaj Adhi Raj calls himself in the letter he lately sent to his suzerain, the Emperor of China. The Hindu's sacred city by the Ganges has often been the resort of political refugees from Nepal, and indeed from every other Hindu principality. Many a desperate and blood-stained conspiracy has been hatched at Benares against a Mayor of the Palace at Khatmandu; and the present enterprise is only one of a long series. In June, Ranbir Jung thought it safer to watch the development of his plot from a distance. His messengers, bearing proclamations sealed with his seal, persuaded four regiments, at a place called Palpa, to mutiny; while in the District of Duncuta they nearly succeeded, with the help of a body of villagers, in capturing the State Treasury. Elsewhere, two smaller treasuries were looted. The movement, however, quickly collapsed, owing, no doubt, to the absence of the real leaders; and the mutineers were more or less severely punished. After being taken in cages to the capital they were sentenced, some to be hanged, and some to penal servitude. The latter sentence would be reserved for Brahmins, whom, in Nepal, it is thought irreligious to kill. It is lawful, however, to shave their heads, thrust pieces of meat—a horrible penalty—into

abundantly clear. A popular and friendly Government in Nepal is needed as much in the interests of our Empire in the East as for the welfare of the Nepalese themselves. The identification of the Indian Government with a usurper who—to satisfy his own ambition, and not, as in other instances in Nepalese history where a Mayor of the Palace has been removed with more or less bloodshed, under orders from a Sovereign, orders given for the safety of the State—waded through the slaughter of honoured relatives to the control of the

---

their mouths, tear the sacred thread from their bodies, and send them to the noisome jungles of the Terai.

Those who watch the politics of Nepal foresaw at the time that if Ranbir Jung and General Jeet Jung took the field themselves, the chances would be all in favour of a successful insurrection. These 'chiefs out of war and statesmen out of place' had a strong following in Nepal, and as the *Pioneer* pointed out, the Administration in office was exceedingly unpopular. The Minister, Bir Shumshere, had incurred the dislike of the people, and still more of the noble class, in many ways. In particular, he had insisted on the Maharajah's sister marrying a man of low birth and bad character. He intended, no doubt, to render the position of royalty in the State still more humiliating; but his policy met with wide disapproval. His absence from the country now, and the sudden appearance of Ranbir Jung, will most likely bring about a rapid and, this time we may hope, bloodless revolution, and lead to a change of Ministry, which we need not regret. A popular as well as a friendly Government is required in Nepal, both in the interests of the people and for the maintenance of satisfactory relations between the Government of India and an important State on the frontier. Nepal supplies the Indian Army with some of its finest soldiers; but our method of recruiting the hardy, gallant Gurkha is still unsatisfactory. The Gurkha finds it difficult to revisit his village when on furlough; his womenfolk are forbidden to accompany him to British India; and he can seldom end his days in his own land. There is reason to believe, moreover, that we have failed so far to enlist recruits from the most warlike tribes, owing to the objections raised by the Nepalese authorities. These and other obstacles to a proper understanding would be removed were the Administration thoroughly well disposed towards us. What is more, the frequent attempts which Russian travellers have made to reach Khatmandu, through Tibet, would lose their significance.

kingdom, is to be deplored, and probably will be followed by consequences detrimental to British rule in the East.

In further proof of the dissatisfaction prevailing in Nepal, it must be added that in the same year (1887) Khurrug, the most energetic of the Shumshere brothers, with Kaisu Sing Thappa, and a few other members of the revolutionary party, also concocted a conspiracy for the Minister's murder. It proved abortive, and Khurrug was deported to Palpa, a penal settlement for political offenders of quality in Nepal. To hoodwink the Indian Government, however, he was ostensibly transferred thither with the rank of Commander-in-Chief of Western Nepal. During the summer of 1889, according to the Indian newspapers, he was on a pilgrimage to Badrinath in British India; but unless Bir Shumshere thinks it expedient to keep up an appearance of fraternal harmony amongst his brothers, it is doubtful whether Khurrug will be permitted to return home. Then there was the attempt made early in 1889 by three of Bir Shumshere's brothers to take his life by poison. This, too, has failed. All these things serve to show that the usurper's life is not worth a moment's purchase. His hand is raised against every man and every man's hand is raised against him, aye, and it would seem the hand of many women also.[1] If the lips of Mr. Girdlestone, Resident

[1] 'It is curious that there should be such persistent rumours abroad of trouble at the Nepalese capital. We heard two or three weeks since a report that Bir Shumshere, the Prime Minister, had died or been killed, and that an effort was being made to keep his death secret for political reasons. Now a report has reached a contemporary via Motihari and Arrah that the Minister was shot by Zenana women, and that "fighting and disturbances are going on at Khatmandu and other places". This is probably only another version of the rumour that reached us in

at Khatmandu during several years, had not been closed in death, the British public might have learnt from him the true character of Bir Shumshere's rule: probably would have so learned, as he was strongly convinced of the impolicy of the Government of India not exercising pressure on behalf of the refugees. Mr. Girdlestone, moreover, could hardly have been silent on the discredit which attaches to the Indian Foreign Office for supporting the murderer of his uncle. Mr. Girdlestone's sympathy for those whose story I tell, largely in the words of documents in the possession of the Indian Government, was very great, and was manifested in various ways. He knew the country and the people well, and had no doubt as to the course, for the sake of justice and for the benefit of the country, which the Government of India should take.

Failing to receive fair and rightful consideration at the hands of the Government of India, these relatives of England's devoted friend of 1857 and of subsequent years make their appeal to England. Far removed from the influences which prevail in Anglo-Indian public life, able to take an impartial view of affairs, mindful of the claims which splendid services frequently spoken of by British Prince and British Viceroy impose upon the British name and honour, Parliament, it is confidently hoped, will not fail in its duty. The eyes of the refugees are turned to Westminster. They pray that on account

more direct fashion three weeks since. If there were any truth in the reports, the Government should have received official information before now from the Resident at Khatmandu; and as no such communication appears to have been received, it would seem that the rumours are untrue.'—*Indian Daily News*, August 16, 1888.

of the claims which they have alike upon India and England—claims founded on services rendered in a terrible crisis and on treaty promises, justice may be done to them and friendship displayed on their behalf. The determination to make an appeal to the British people and Parliament was decided after a family council, at which the following memorial to Her Royal Highness SRI PANCH, DOWAGER JAITA MAHARANI OF NEPAL, was unanimously adopted:—

May it please your Royal Highness,

With profound deference and submission, we, the undersigned, beg to approach your Royal Highness with this humble representation, expressive of our deep disappointment at the ungenerous treatment which we have experienced at the hands of the Government of India. After the treacherous murder of our universally beloved Prime Minister, Maharajah Sir Ranadip Sing, and the usurpation of power by Bir Shumshere and his brothers, we were induced to come to British India in the confident hope of receiving every assistance from our powerful ally in rescuing our country from the hands of the usurpers. That hope was based—

1st. On the services which Nepal had rendered to the Government of India during the Indian Mutiny;

and,

2ndly. On the third clause of our Treaty with the British Government (No. XLVIII of 1801), which provides 'that the principals and officers of both Governments will cordially consider the friends and enemies of either State to be the friends and enemies of the other; and this consideration must ever remain permanent and in force, from generation to generation.'

But our hope was doomed to bitter disappointment. Within about two months of the cruel murder of Maharajah Sir Ranadip Sing, the Government of India, perhaps at the instance of a new Resident, wholly unacquainted with the country and the real sentiments of the people, and before we had hardly any opportunity of stating our case, precipitately recognised Bir Shumshere as Prime Minister, and entered into political relations with him as the rightful representative of the Nepal Durbar. On our arrival in British territory, memorials were submitted to the Viceroy and Governor General of India in Council on behalf of our country, and also for the restoration of our property, both personal and immovable; but our representations have been altogether unheeded, and we have been subjected to a most galling police espionage as if *we* were the enemies of both States. The Government of India, which is never slow to insist on the observance of treaty obligations on the part of its allies, has shown its singular fidelity to Nepal by taking the part of the unscrupulous traitor.

Meanwhile, the country is being ground down under the iron heel of Bir Shumshere. There have been repeated massacres of innocent men since his usurpation of power; nearly all the nobility and trusted leaders of the people have been either killed or forced into exile, and their property seized by him; there is no security of life and property, justice being polluted at its very fount; trade and every industrial enterprise are being fast ruined by systematic oppression, and by jealous restrictions imposed on free intercourse between Nepal and the rest of India; the public revenue is wasted in promoting either the personal indulgence or the self-aggrandisement of the usurper, whose arbitrary will constitutes the law of the land; and the entire nation is utterly demoralised by a policy of stern repression, and emasculated by the deprivation of all means of successful resistance to tyranny. And who can say, now that the pillars of the State and the natural defenders of the throne have been removed, that Bir Shumshere will not, in the pursuit of his lawless ambition, crown his supreme guilt and infamy by ultimate regicide?

Under these circumstances, we humbly but most earnestly pray, that your Royal Highness will be graciously pleased, on behalf of our ancient kingdom, to make an appeal under the existing treaty to the People and the Parliament of Great Britain. England is no less just and generous than great and powerful among the nations of the earth; and we are sanguine that the moment her sympathies are awakened in favour of Nepal, the downfall of the tyrant is certain. We would ask the British

Government, in fulfilment of its treaty engagements, to withhold its support from Bir Shumshere, and to assist us in establishing a regency, composed of the senior members of the Royal family, to conduct the administration of the State during the minority of our beloved sovereign. Such a regency, we are sure, would be most acceptable to all classes of the people, as being in entire harmony with precedents in our past history, and calculated to ensure the speedy restoration of internal peace and tranquillity by vesting the supreme authority of the State in those who are naturally entitled to our allegiance and veneration. And we are confident that if, under British auspices, your Royal Highness, attended by your faithful Sirdars, now appeared with a small force in Nepal, the army and the people—by this time wholly disillusionised—would readily flock to your Royal Highness's standard, and throw off the hated yoke of Bir Shumshere with heartfelt alacrity and with feelings of deep gratitude to their British deliverers.

With sentiments of profound loyalty and reverence,

We remain,

Your Royal Highness's most devoted and humble servants,

(sd.) PADAM JUNG RANA BAHADUR,

(sd.) DHOJI NURSING RANA BAHADUR,

and others.

The points, shorn of all adventitious circumstances, upon which the opinion of Parliament and the goodwill of the British people are besought, are three in number, and are of the simplest character.

1st. Whether, under the existing treaty, our Government is or is not bound to interfere actively in favour of the Maharani and the exiled Princes?

2ndly. Whether, having regard to the signal services rendered to us during the Mutiny by Maharajahs Jung Bahadur and Ranadip Sing, and the numerous proofs of friendship towards our Government they furnished during their lifetime, we are not morally bound to help their families and children in their present unfortunate position?

3rdly. Is it good and sound policy to uphold a usurper, stained with the deepest guilt, in opposition to the wishes of the principal members of the Royal family and of the leading men of Nepal?

There can be but one answer to these questions, and that, I think, entirely in favour of these friends of Britain in India, friends who so far have been treated with the scantiest consideration throughout and with positive discourtesy and unkindness on special occasions. So far as their own country people are concerned, if a plebiscite were taken to-day in Nepal, the whole land, I am credibly assured, with the exception of the immediate partizans of Bir Shumshere—not a large number—would unhesitatingly vote against him. British-Indian support alone maintains him in power. But for that support he would long before this have fallen a victim to the wild justice which is so characteristic of the Himalayan Highlanders.

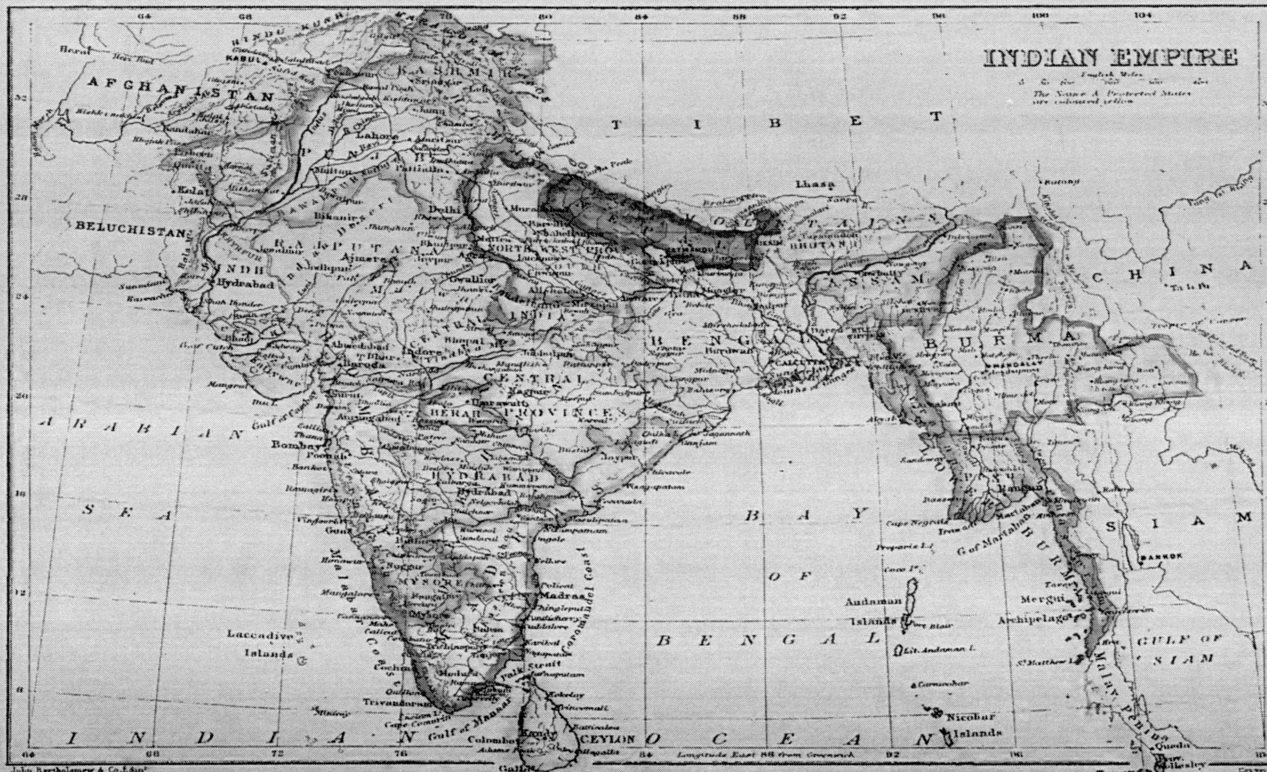
INDIAN EMPIRE
The Native & Protected States are coloured yellow
AFGHANISTAN
BELUCHISTAN
TIBET
CHINA
SIAM
BURMA
ASSAM
BHOTAN
BENGAL
CENTRAL INDIA
CENTRAL PROVINCES
BERAR
HYDRABAD
MYSORE
RAJPUTANA
SINDH
KASHMIR
NORTH WEST PROV.
ARABIAN SEA
BAY OF BENGAL
INDIAN OCEAN
GULF OF SIAM
CEYLON
Andaman Islands
Nicobar Islands
Laccadive Islands
Bombay
Madras
Calcutta
Delhi
Lahore
Hydrabad
Lhasa
Bangkok
Penang
Colombo
Kandy
Mergui Archipelago
Coromandel Coast
Gulf of Manaar
Gulf of Martaban
Longitude East 88 from Greenwich
John Bartholomew & Co., Edin.

CHAPTER I.

THE KINGDOM OF NEPAL.[1]

The independent kingdom of Nepal is included in the southern ranges of the Himalayas, beyond the northern boundary of British India.[2] It lies with an inclination from north-west to south-east, and is comprised within the north latitudes 26°-25′ and 30°-17′, and lengthwise, between east longitudes 80°-6′ and 88°-14.′ Its greatest length is about 512 miles, its breadth varies from 70 to 150 miles, and it has a total area of about 54,000 square miles. A desolate and uninhabited tract divides it from Tibet on the north; the Kálí or Sarda river bounds it on the west, and on the south-west and south the British Districts of Pilibhit, Kheri, Bahráich, Gonda, Busti, Gorakhpore, Champáran, Muzaffarpur, Darbhanga, Bhágalpur, and Purniah constitute a boundary line which runs at varying distances from the foot of the Himalayas, sometimes to within thirty miles of it. On the east, Nepal is bounded by the Mechi river, the Singatha ridge, and the hill principality of Sikkim.

---

[1] The particulars contained in this chapter, and in subsequent chapters so far as they relate to the past history of Nepal, are founded on 'Sketches from Nepal', by Dr. J. Oldfield, 2 vols. (W. H. Allen and Co., 1880), and Sir W. W. Hunter's Gazetteer of India, Art., NEPAL.

[2] See map facing this page.

The physical aspect of the country is extremely diversified. Its loftiest peak is Mount Everest, with an elevation of 29,002 ft., the highest known summit of the globe, while almost the whole of its northern mountain wall is above the line of perpetual snow. All the highest tops stand to the south of the elevated ground which forms the southern watershed of the Sanpu, or great river of Tibet. The peaks are connected with the water-shed, and from them start cross-spurs which serve as barriers to the three great river basins of the Kurnali, the Gandak, and the Kosi. These basins have a southward slope, contracting as they proceed towards the plains and the watershed along the huge ridges of Api, Diwàlagiri, Gosainthan, and Kanchanjanga; these give rise to several groups of mountain streams which, as they converge and unite, swell the volume of the three main rivers mentioned above. The little stream of Bagmati waters the valley of Khatmandu, and the drainage of the Terái is for the most part of purely local origin. In this labyrinth of mountains and rivers are situate the extensive valleys of Sumla, Khatmandu, Pokhra, Dhang, Deskhm, and Chitawan, enjoying in their terraced elevation a diversity of climate ranging from the heat of the plains to the cold of perpetual snow. The valley of Khatmandu, 4,000 ft. above sea-level, is of oval shape; the maximum length and breadth are 20 and 15 miles respectively; and, although it is in no higher latitude than 27°-35′ to 27°-50′ north, it has the climate of the south of Europe.[1]

[1] Dr. Oldfield (vol. i., pp. 72—74) gives an interesting description of the valley of Nepal, a valley almost as full of interest as the Vale of Kashmir. He writes :—'According to the tradition of all Hindus, what

As no regular census has ever been taken of the country, the population of Nepal is variously estimated at from two to five millions and a-half, the former figure being supposed to be nearer the truth. The chief administrative divisions are:—In the hills: Baitari, Doti and Acham, Tumla, Satiana, Dhang and Deskhm, Palpa and Pokhra, Gurkha and Khatmandu, Sindhulia, Dhankuta, Ilam. In the Terái: Nayá Mulk ('new territory'), Batwál, Newalpur and Chitawan, Pursa Bara and Rotahat, Sirlahi and Mihtari, Suptari, and Murang. All these districts, as a rule, are governed by Gurkhalí officers.

Rent is seldom fixed by competition in the various systems of land tenure in Nepal. The Crown lands lie chiefly in the Gurkha territory, though there is hardly any district in which the King has not some land of his own. The husbandmen who till it get a share of the

---

is now the valley of Nepal was, in the early ages of the world, a large and very deep lake, of an oval form, and encircled by lofty mountains, which rose more or less precipitously from its edges. Manjusri Bodhisatwa has the credit of having converted this lake into a dry valley, by cutting through Mount Kotbar on its southern side with his sword, and so making a passage through which all the waters escaped. The cleft in the mountain, caused by Manjusri's sword, remains to the present time, and constitutes the pass or channel between the Phulchoah and Champadevi hills, through which the Bagmati river leaves the Valley of Nepal. There is good reason to believe that this legend is based upon truth, and that Nepal was in remote ages a mountain lake, enclosed in the hollow of the same circular range of hills by which the valley is surrounded at the present day. It is probable that in consequence either of one of those subterranean convulsions common to all mountain districts, or of the gradual but continuous elevation of its bottom, or from both causes combined, the lake burst its boundaries on its southern side, and that a large portion of its waters escaped into the lower hills through the channel which is now the bed of the Bagmati river. At the same time that its waters were being slowly drained off, the hollow of the lake must have been gradually filled up by the soil constantly

produce, while in other cases the feudal system of enforced gratuitous service on the part of the tenant is observed. The expenses of the royal household are defrayed from this source. In Nepal, as in India generally, Brahmans occupy rent-free lands, the gift of royalty; they are absolute owners of their property, the commission of certain crimes only entailing a forfeiture. On the accession of each Prince the Newar landholders are obliged to renew their lease, paying a heavy premium on such occasions. The army as a rule is annually billeted on the land.

The variety of Nepal climate is best manifest in the agricultural produce of the country. What with its rugged soil and the backward condition of the people, even the primeval ploughs and the village cart are rarities. Yet the country is most rich in its vegetable products. Among timber trees, the *Terai sál* is well known and extensively used all over Bengal. It is of great value for sleepers and house beams, owing to its dura-

---

brought into it by numberless streams from the sides of the surrounding mountains. These processes of draining off and filling up must have gone on slowly, steadily, and simultaneously, so as to allow of the uniform deposition along the bottom of the lake of all the soil and solid ingredients which were contained within its waters. In the course of time these deposits became more and more consolidated, until at length, the waters having dried up or drained away, the entire mountain hollow became filled up with a mass of alluvial soil, the extent of which corresponded with the limits, as its surface did with the level, of the former lake. This view of the formation of the valley is confirmed by numerous facts which can hardly be explained by any other theory. At the present day the continuity of the mountain barrier around the valley is so perfect, that were it possible by any means to block up that one pass through which the Bahmati river flows towards the plains, not one drop of water could escape by any other channel, and, in the course of time, the accumulation of its pent-up waters would convert the valley again into a lake.'

bility, strength, straightness, and size. A *sál* beam, as sound after a century as when it was first cut out of its parent tree, is not an uncommon sight in many a Bengal household. There is, besides, the Mimosa, from which the catechu of commerce is derived, the *sisu*, and the *bhanja*, the wood of which is in much request for cart axles. Cotton trees, acacias, and tree figs are not infrequent. The hill forests contain oak, holly, rhododendron, maple, chestnut, walnut, *champa*, hornbeam, pines, and firs in abundance; but the want of carriage facilities in consequence of the inaccessible nature of the country render them, all but locally, valueless. Almost side by side with the oaks and pines of colder latitudes are to be seen the rattans and bamboos of the tropics; and while the peach, the raspberry, the walnut, the mulberry, and every variety of European fruits and vegetables all seem to grow wild in the country, the warmer valleys are rich with a good and abundant crop of the pine apple. The land is very fertile, and in some districts so much as three crops are grown in the year: wheat or barley, or buck wheat or mustard, in the winter, radishes or garlic or potatoes in the spring, and Indian corn, rice, or pepper, during the rains. Ginger is a valuable product in the hill tracts; and besides various pulses and cereals, mustard, madder, sugar cane and cardamoms are also grown. Amongst the spontaneous productions of the soil are the cherry and the tea tree, the laurel, the alder, the willow, and the oleander. Several edible roots and herbs also grow wild, and form a considerable part of the sustenance of the poorer inhabitants; many medicinal plants, woods yielding the richest dyes, and the well known intoxicant *charas* are also among the agricultural produce of the country.

Nepal is the home of almost all the wild animals for which India is famous. The elephant, rhinoceros, tiger, and leopard abound in the Terái; deer are common throughout the country; and the Nepal sheep is famous for its considerable size and fine wool. Beautiful birds are also to be seen, particularly pheasants of golden and spotted plumage. The mineral wealth of the country is also not inconsiderable. Iron ore is found near the surface, and is not surpassed in purity by that of any other country. Sulphur and copper are easy of access and equally abundant. A great variety of stones is to be met with, particularly jasper and marble, as well as limestone and slate. Among the manufactures of the country are iron and copper wares, cotton and woollen cloths, and brass and bell-metal. One bell manufactured at Bhatgaon measured 5ft. in diameter. The Newars, who are almost the only artizans in Nepal, have also a knowledge of carpentry; it is remarkable that they never use a saw, dividing their wood, when of any size, by a chisel and mallet. Their manufacture of packing paper is also very interesting: they make the paper out of the bark of a shrub—the bark being very strong and of exceptional stoutness.

The only two countries which have a commercial relationship with Nepal are Tibet on the north, and British India on the south. The Tibetan exchanges *pashmina* or shawl wool, salt, borax, musk, quicksilver, and gold-dust for the Nepalese metal wares, while European piece goods and hardware and Indian cotton goods and spices also find their way beyond the Himalayas. The Indian trade is carried on along a frontier line of seven hundred miles; and though a considerable portion of the Imperial revenue consists of transit duties, they are, as a rule, heavy in the case of luxuries and lighter in the case of necessaries. On each of the trade routes there is a toll station, and the tolls are sometimes farmed out by public auction. There is a duty on every article, both for export and import, which is said to be not oppressive; and goods are rated promiscuously according to their character, their value, weight, load, or number. The principal articles of export from Nepal are the following: Rice and inferior grains, oil seeds, *ghi* or clarified butter, honey, cattle, falcons for hawking, *mainás* or parrots, timber, opium, musk, *chiretta*, borax, madder, turpentine, catechu or cutch, jute, hides, and furs, dried ginger, cardamoms, red chillies, turmeric, and yak-tails. The chief imports are: raw cotton, cotton twist, and cotton piece goods (both Indian and European), woollen cloth, shawls, rugs, flannel, silk, brocade, embroidery, sugar, spices, indigo, tobacco, areca-nut, vermilion, lac, oils, salt, a little fine rice, buffaloes, sheep and goats, sheet copper, copper and brass ornaments, beads, mirrors, precious stones, guns and gunpowder for sporting purposes, tea from Kumáun and Dárjíling. There is no possible means of ascertaining the aggregate value of this trade, the difficulty from want of proper statistical machinery being enhanced from the small bulk and high value of many of the articles in transit. Recently attempts have been made to furnish the required information; and these give a total of £1,686,000 for the registered trade of Nepal both ways in 1877-78, and of £2,176,263 for the same trade in 1882-83. 'The gain to British traders', says Sir W. W. Hunter, 'engaged in the traffic between the North-Western Provinces and Nepal, is officially estimated at £100,000 yearly.'

Of the Himalayan Highlanders, now under Nepalese rule, less is known than, perhaps, of any Asiatics save the Tibetans. Dr. Oldfield gives the reason for this in a description of the features of the country and the characteristics of the people (vol. i, chap. xxi). He says :—'In the middle of the eighteenth century, when the British under Lord Clive were with difficulty establishing a firm footing in Bengal, that portion of the Himalayas which is now consolidated into the compact kingdom of Nepal was broken up into a number of petty principalities and small independent States, which, though constantly warring among themselves, had little or no connection with the plains of Hindustan. The vast tract of forest and of marshy malarious land which skirts, almost uninterruptedly, the southern face of the Himalayas, from Assam in the far east almost to the Sutlej in the north-west, formed an insuperable bar to any regular intercourse between the nations of the plains and those of the hills.

'Thus isolated from connection with Hindustan, the hill Rajahs and their subjects became, as it were, "a peculiar people". Absorbed in their own internal affairs—at one time warring with neighbouring chiefs, at another occupied in pastoral pursuits, or in hunting expeditions within their own territories—they knew little and cared less about the political changes and revolutions which were occurring in Bengal. Inhabiting a cool and bracing climate, they were physically far superior to the languid and enervated Bengalees. The virgin purity of their native soil had never been sullied by the foot of the foreign invader; they were the only Hindu State which had not been degraded by Muhammadan conquest. Morally, therefore, as well as physically, they looked, and they still look, upon themselves as superior to any of the Hindus in the plains. These feelings induced a proud independence and energy of character, almost unknown in other parts of India. These mountaineers, one and all, were Hindus on principle and by descent; but they refused to be hampered by all the bigotry and prejudices of Brahmanical law. While they retained the substance, they rejected much of the shadow of Hinduism, and openly disregarded many observances which were and are considered as essential by the more orthodox professors of that religion in the plains. Such conduct naturally gave great offence. The Hindu of the Himalayas began to be looked on by the Hindu of the plains very much in the same light that the Protestant is looked upon by the Roman Catholic. As the orthodox Roman Catholic calls the Protestant a "heretic", so the orthodox Brahman of Benares calls his brother Hindu of Nepal a "Pariah". These various differences in religion, in customs, in occupations, and in language, engendered great bitterness of feeling between the races of the plains and the races of the hills. The bigoted Hindus of Bengal held very little intercourse with the proud independent mountaineers whom they regarded as "aliens in religion, aliens in language, and aliens in blood". The hill tribes throughout the Himalayas — the natives of Sikkim, of Kiranti, of Nepal, of Gurkha, of Palpa, of Doti, of Kumáun, of Garhwal, and of Sarmur — saw their Hindu countrymen of the plains one after another subdued by a handful of British soldiery; but, undisturbed in the seclusion of their own mountain fastnesses, they were indifferent spectators to the struggles which were going on, and never directly or indirectly interfered or offered to assist in stemming the tide of European conquest. This neutrality on their part with respect to the general politics of India was the result, not of any system of policy, but of their feeling that they were so shut out by natural and, as they considered, impenetrable barriers from the rest of the world, that they felt no interest in the momentous struggle which was revolutionizing Hindustan.

'The people of the plains regarded the hill tribes in the same manner. They felt no interest in their movements. They looked on the sturdy mountaineers as formidable in their own hills, but as not dangerous elsewhere. The vast forests and the malarious terai beyond which they lived would, they knew, prevent the hillmen from making incursions, beyond mere border forays, into the plains. They knew that the vast mountain regions extending from the Brahmaputra to the Sutlej were as inhospitable as they were extensive; that the towns were but few, the population poor, but yet such as were to be dreaded when fighting in defence of their hearths and homes; in fact, they were fully aware that there was nothing in the whole tract to tempt their cupidity, to gratify their love of plunder, or to repay them for the dangers and hardships of mountain warfare.

'The natives of the plains, therefore, although they could not altogether ignore the existence of the hill tribes, yet looked on them politically as *hors de combat.* The indifference which the hillmen displayed towards the politics of Hindustan was, therefore abundantly returned by the natives of the plains, who felt utterly unconcerned in the fierce contests which were constantly occurring, especially towards the middle and close of the eighteenth century, between rival hill Rajahs of whose names even they were ignorant, or between petty principalities of whose existence they were hardly aware.

'It is in a great measure owing to this feeling of indifference that we now know so little of the separate and individual States of which this vast mountain republic, extending over territory upwards of eight hundred miles in length, was composed. The names even of many of them are forgotten; the origin of the State of Gurkha, the most warlike and powerful among them, is little better than conjectural; and of the Newar kingdom of Nepal itself—the most important, the most populous, and the most highly civilized of them all, and the only one which had any regular intercourse with the plains—we cannot say we know with certainty anything of its annals, or of its people, until towards the close of the eighteenth century, when, the British power being firmly established in Bengal, the last prince of the Newar dynasty, in his last efforts against Gurkha aggressions, appealed to our arms for aid in expelling the Gurkha invader from the valley of Nepal.'

In 1851 Jung Bahadur, when pressed to make a

good road from the plains of India to the valley of Nepal, stated that the prejudices of his countrymen were very strong against this being done: they thought that while the roads remained in their present condition no invading army could make its way to the valley. For his own part, he said, since he had been to England and had seen English railroads, tunnels, etc., he knew our power and skill so well that he was convinced, if we could not make a road over a mountain, we should make a tunnel under it, so that no mountain could stop our progress. 'But,' he added, 'though the cat cannot fight on even terms with the lion, yet if the lion drives the cat into a corner the cat will scratch his eyes.'

In so remarking the great Nepalese Minister was only expressing the views of his countrymen. 'Now, equally as in the days of Bhim Sen', says Dr. Oldfield,[1] 'the Nepalese Durbar wish to have nothing to do with us. At the point of the bayonet they were forced to yield to the establishment of a British Resident at their Court;[2] but they would be as delighted now as they would have been immediately after the war, if they could dispense with the presence of that functionary among them. They know, however, that the withdrawal of the Resident would be immediately followed by the resumption of the Terai lands, and the probable conquest and annexation of their country. They submit, therefore, without further complaint, to a state of things which

[1] Vol. i, pp. 300, 301.

[2] At Makwanpur, General Ochterlony, by Lord Hastings' express command, told the Gurkha Vakils that all other points of the treaty were more or less open to subsequent discussion, but that 'they must take either the Resident or war'. They yielded, and Lieutenant Boileau was sent as *locum tenens* until the arrival of the Resident.

they cannot alter. Although they are still as insuperably averse as ever to any kind of intimate connection with the British Government, yet this aversion does not depend on any actual feeling of hostility towards us. But they look on us as dangerous and encroaching neighbours, and judging from the experience and fate of other States throughout India, they are firmly convinced that if once the British gain a footing (even though it be of a friendly character) within the Valley of Nepal, from that time the knell of their national independence will have struck. Acting on these principles, they distrust, and ever have distrusted, every friendly overture that is made to them; they throw obstacles in the way of anything like extensive intercourse between the two nations, and they carry their suspicions of our interested motives to such a degree, that they will not even allow a single European to travel through their hills for the purpose of collecting purely scientific information. Nothing will ever disabuse them of the belief that the British are anxious to conquer and annex Nepal. They acknowledge our supremacy in the plains, and they think that the only way to prevent that supremacy from being established in Nepal as well as in Hindustan is to keep us at a distance, and by isolating themselves from all intimate connection with us, avoid giving us the opportunity of gratifying what they consider the national love of foreign aggrandisement. These considerations form the real and only key to the very exclusive policy which Nepal has systematically adopted towards the British Government from the date of the last war up to the present time.'

The army of Nepal, computed to be 30,000 strong,

consists of 13,000 militia and 17,000 regulars. They cost the State £400,000 annually, land of which value is permanently allotted for the purpose. As soldiers they have always rendered efficient service to the British at various periods of history. The excellence and value of this service will be demonstrated later in these pages.

Little is known of the early history of Nepal. Like that of most other Eastern countries, it fades into misty fables, vanishing back thousands of years. It never owned allegiance to the Great Mogul, and beyond that Hari Sing, one of the Princes of Oudh, completely subdued it in 1323 A.D., nothing is known of the Himalayan kingdom during the long period of Mahommedan rule in India. The Gurkhas, under Prithwi Nárâyan conquered the country in 1760 A.D., and in less than a year made themselves masters of the whole valley. The failure of Captain Kinloch to enter Nepal at the head of a British force, defying its Terái fever without and its rugged hills within, dates about this period. Prithwi Nárâyan died in 1717, leaving two sons, Sing Pratap and Bahadur Shah, the Regent Murray of Nepal. During his regency over the infant son of his elder brother whom he had placed on the throne, the dominions of Nepal extended from the Mechi river on the east to the Garhwál district on the west, and from the border of Tibet to the border of Hindustan.

The cupidity of the Nepalese towards the close of the administration of Warren Hastings led their predatory hordes into Tibet, and thus brought them into contact with its suzerain, the Emperor of China. In 1790 a Chinese army 70,000 strong marched against Nepal and threatened its capital, Khatmandu

A peace, humiliating to the Nepalese, was at length concluded; they had to acknowledge the suzerainty of China and restore their Tibetan booty. There is no record, however, of any tribute ever being demanded by China or paid. In 1792 Lord Cornwallis laid the first foundation of a commercial treaty with the Gurkhalís; it fell through shortly, however, owing to their apathy and indifference. In 1795 the minor king entered upon his twentieth year, and surprised his uncle by demanding to rule in person. For one year he reigned with exemplary virtue and tact; but at the end of that period he completely gave himself up to profligacy and vice. In tyranny he surpassed the worst tyrant of the East. He had a son by a Brahman widow, and he abdicated his throne in favour of this illegitimate boy. On the death of his mistress he completely lost what little of sanity was yet left in him; and the recollection of his frantic atrocities gives a shudder to this day to the Nepalese. Temples were ordered to be demolished and the golden images therein to be ground to dust; and when the Hindu soldiery refused to obey such sacrilegious orders boiling oil was ordered to be poured over their naked bodies to teach them obedience. A conspiracy was at length formed against the tyrant; he found himself unable to cope with it, and under cover of night fled to Benares in May, 1800. The appearance of Ran Bahadur Shah, the Nepalese king, within British dominions, was eagerly taken advantage of by the Indian Government, who were long waiting for such an opportunity; and a treaty having been concluded with the exiled king by Captain W. D. Knox, he proceeded to Khatmandu as the first British Ambassador in 1802.

This second treaty proved no better than the first, and the jealousy of the Nepalese officers compelled the withdrawal of the Residency in 1804. By the clever management of his wife, whom he uniformly illtreated, Ran Bahadur Shah had, in the meantime, succeeded in regaining his throne; but a recurrence of his former atrocities inflamed the whole nobility, and he was put to death in 1805. Nepal was about this time deluged with the noblest blood in the land; the opposite factions fought to their last man almost; and an insignificant remnant of straggling survivors succeeded at length in placing the sole remaining son of the last king on the throne.

Strange as it may seem, despite these sanguinary convulsions that were tearing their court and capital for such a long time, the Nepalese army was steadily extending its conquest from the valley of the Ganges on the east to the far-west shores of the Sutlej. The invaders fortified Almorá, Srínagar, and Maláun, wrenched half Sikkim from its King, and meeting with a check in their northern progress by the army of China and the still more impenetrable barriers of the Northern Himalayas, thought of giving vent to their military ardour by an expedition to the south, where the fertile plains under the protectorate of an unknown power could not but whet their cupidity. A series of depredations followed; and when the British Government remonstrated against these unjust aggressions on their territory, a Joint Commission was instituted to adjudicate on the rival claims. The award being in favour of the British, a European detachment was sent to take possession of the debateable land; but on the retirement of the army to its autumn quarters, the Nepalese fell on the English out-posts and drove them back with terrible slaughter. In 1814 war was declared, and an English army entered the dominion of the Gurkhas through the more accessible routes on its western frontier, between the valleys of the Jumna and Sutlej. The first year's campaign was extremely disastrous to the English army. The enemy offered a most desperate resistance at Kalunga, near Dehra; and here, while leading his army to the charge, General Gillespie fell. Next year Sir David Ochterlony, who had assumed charge of the army, completely changed the aspect of affairs. He had 33,000 men under him; and he marched with this army upon the Nepalese capital. He met with an obstinate resistance from the Gurkhas, and still worse hindrance in the mountain fastnesses. When the English army encamped at length within three days' march of Khatmandu, the Nepal Durbar decided upon treating with the invaders. A convention was drawn up on the 4th of March, 1816, in which the Nepalese undertook to give up all claims to the territory in dispute, and to renounce all their conquests to the west of the Kali river. China, too, played a part in this contest. When sore pressed by the army, the Nepalese naturally looked to their pseudo-suzerain for help; but the Chinese declined to render them any support. Further reflection on the impertinence of a vassal who had engaged in foreign wars without the consent of his lord, roused the Celestial wrath, however, to move an army of 15,000 strong into the country of the Gurkhas; but the timely mediation of Nepalese officers at the Court of Pekin, who were deputed for the purpose, arrested further calamity to the little kingdom.

In 1816, the boy who had succeeded to the throne of his father, Ran Bahadur Shah, died of small-pox. He left one son, Rajendra Bikram Shah, who now ascended the throne of Nepal at the age of three. The chief figure in Nepal history from this time forth is the late Prime Minister, Sir Jung Bahadur. But the career of this splendid soldier, patriotic statesman, and staunch ally of the English, must be reserved for a fresh chapter.

CHAPTER II.

A FRIEND IN NEED.

During the storm and stress of the Sepoy Mutiny in 1857, Nepal showed, in the most practical of all ways, her good-will towards the Government of India. Colonel Malleson has described, in the fourth volume of his history of the Mutiny,[1] the way in which this good-will was displayed. The centre of the revolt was in those Provinces of North-Western Bengal and Oudh which bordered upon the Kingdom of Nepal. That country for seven hundred miles runs conterminous with British territories. Its Gurkha troops are famed for their devoted courage and for their hardihood, these qualities constituting them the very flower of Eastern soldiery. For many years friendship had existed between the Indian Government and the Himalayan Kingdom. In 1801 a treaty was concluded between the King of Nepal and the Marquis of Wellesley, then Governor-

[1] In reply to a request made to them, Messrs. W. H. Allen and Co., the well-known publishers to the India Office and of works on India, have courteously permitted me to quote the passages from the history of the Mutiny, which, in this chapter, tell the story of the services of the Nepalese Contingent.

General of India.[1] For the purposes of the story to be told in these pages two articles of the Treaty acquire peculiar significance. The first of these articles is No. III. 'The principals and officers of both Governments', it states, 'will cordially consider the friends and enemies of either State to be the friends and enemies of the other; and this consideration must ever remain permanent and in force, from generation to generation.' The final stipulation runs thus:—'It is incumbent upon the principals and officers mutually

---

[1] No. XLVIII.

TREATY WITH THE RAJAH OF NEPAL, 1801.

Whereas it is evident as the noonday sun to the enlightened understanding of exalted nobles and of powerful chiefs and rulers, that Almighty God has entrusted the protection and government of the universe to the authority of princes, who make justice their principle, and that by the establishment of a friendly connection between them universal happiness and prosperity is secured, and that the more intimate the relation of amity and union the greater is the general tranquility; in consideration of these circumstances, His Excellency the Most Noble the Governor-General, Marquis Wellesley, etc., etc., and the Maha Rajah have established a system of friendship between the respective Governments of the Company and the Rajah of Nepal, and have agreed to the following articles:—

ARTICLE I.

It is necessary and incumbent upon the principals and officers of the two Governments constantly to exert themselves to improve the friendship subsisting between the two States, and to be zealously and sincerely desirous of the prosperity and success of the Government and subjects of both.

ARTICLE II.

The incendiary and turbulent representations of the disaffected who are the disturbers of our mutual friendship, shall not be attended to without investigation and proof.

ARTICLE III.

The principals and officers of both Governments will cordially consider the friends and enemies of either State to be the friends and enemies of the other; and this consideration must ever remain permanent and in force, from generation to generation.

to abide by the spirit of this Treaty, which is now drawn out according to their faith and religion, and, deeming it in force from generation to generation, that they should not deviate from it ; and any person who may transgress against it will be punished by Almighty God, both in this world and in a future state'. No Indian Treaty contains more emphatic stipulations, binding the respective parties to the exercise of greater amity and more good-will one towards another.

ARTICLE IV.

If any one of the neighbouring powers of the either State should commence any altercation, or dispute, and design, without provocation, unjustly to possess himself of the territories of either country, and should entertain hostile intentions with the view of taking that country, the Vakeels on the part of our respective Governments at either Court will fully report all particulars to the head of the State, who, according to the obligations of friendship subsisting between the two States, after having heard the said particulars, will give whatever answer and advice may be proper.

ARTICLE V.

Whenever any dispute of boundary and territory between the two countries may arise, such dispute shall be decided through our respective Vakeels, or our officers, according to the principles of justice and right; and a landmark shall be placed upon the said boundary, and which shall constantly remain, that the officers both now and hereafter may consider it as a guide and not make any encroachment.

ARTICLE VI.

Such places as are upon the frontiers of the dominions of the Noble Vizier and of Nepal, and respecting which any dispute may arise, such dispute shall be settled by the mediation of the Vakeel on the part of the Company, and in the presence of one from the Nepal Government, and one from his Excellency the Vizier.

ARTICLE VII.

So many elephants, on account of Muckanacinpoor, are annually sent to the Company by the Rajah of Nepal; and therefore the Governor-General, with a view of promoting the satisfaction of the Rajah of Nepal, and in consideration of the improved friendly connection, and of this new treaty, relinquishes and foregoes the tribute above mentioned, and directs that the officers of the Company, both now and hereafter,

So far as the particular aim of this work is concerned, the Treaty-Articles quoted are of special value and significance. 'We cannot bring any pressure, friendly or otherwise', says the Foreign Secretary, in effect, to the royal and other refugees, when they appeal to him; it is not in our power to do so. Yet, it will be seen by a perusal of the Treaty itself that its largest provision has relation to exactly that kind of pressure. The Indian Government actually safeguards by Treaty arrangements of the character of

---

from generation to generation, shall never, during the continuance of the engagement contracted by the treaty, (so long as the conditions of this treaty shall be in force), exact the elephants from the Rajah.

ARTICLE VIII.

If any of the defendants or inhabitants of either country should fly and take refuge in the other, and a requisition should be made for such persons on the part of the Nepal Government by its constituted Vakeel in attendance on the Governor-General, or on the part of the Company's Government by its representative residing at Nepal, it is, in this case, mutually agreed, that if such person should have fled after transgressing the laws of his Government, it is incumbent upon the principals of both Governments immediately to deliver him up to the Vakeel at their respective courts, that he may be sent in perfect security to the frontier of their respective territories.

ARTICLE IX.

The Maha Rajah of Nepal agrees that a pergunnah, with all the lands attached to it, excepting privileged lands and those appropriated to religious purposes, and to jaghires, etc., which are specified separately in the account of collections, shall be given up to Samee Jeo for his expenses, as a present. The conditions with respect to Samee Jeo are, that if he should remain at Benares, or at any other place within the Company's provinces, and should spontaneously farm his jaghire to the officers of Nepal, in that event the amount of collections shall be punctually paid to him, agreeably to certain kists which may be hereafter settled; that he may appropriate the same to his necessary expenses, and that he may continue in religious abstraction, according to his agreement, which he had engraved on brass, at the time of his abdication of the Roy, and of his resigning it in my favour. Again, in the event of his establishing his residence in his jaghire, and of his realising

those for which the Dowager Queen of Nepal and the son of Sir Jung Bahadur make request, requests which are pooh-poohed as though they were outside the comity of nations. Personal obligations are even more callously, not to say superciliously, ignored. In this respect Lord Lansdowne at Quetta and his Foreign Secretary in Calcutta are at opposite poles of thought and practice. There should be identity of thought and practice in such a matter, and the Viceroy's views ought to prevail.

At the time when the Mutiny broke out at Meerut,

---

the collections through his own officers, it is proper that he should not keep such a one and other disaffected persons in his service; and besides one hundred men and maid servants, etc, he must not entertain any persons as soldiers, with a view to the collection of the revenue of the pergunnah; and to the protection of his person he may take two hundred soldiers of the forces of the Nepal government, the allowances of whom shall be paid by the Rajah of Nepal. He must be cautious, also, of commencing altercation, either by speech or writing: neither must he give protection to the rebellious and fugitives of the Nepal country; nor must he commit plunder and devastation upon the subjects of Nepal. In the event of such delinquency being proved, to the satisfaction of the two Governments, the aid and protection of the Company shall be withdrawn from him; and in that event, also, it shall be at the option of the Rajah of Nepal, whether or not he will confiscate his jaghire.

The Maharajah also agrees, on his part, that if Samee Jeo should take up his residence within the Company's provinces, and should farm out his land to the officers of Nepal, and that the kists should not be paid according to agreement or that he should fix his residence on his jaghire, and any of the inhabitants of Nepal should give him or the ryots of his pergunnah any molestation, a requisition shall be made by the Governor-General of the Company on this subject to the Rajah. The Governor-General is security for the Rajah's performance of this condition, and the Maha Rajah will immediately acquit himself of the requisition of the Governor-General agreeably to what is above written. If any profits should arise in the collection of the said pergunnah, in consequence of the activity of the officers, or any defalcation occur from their inattention, in either case the Rajah of Nepal will be totally unconcerned.

ARTICLE X.

With the view of carrying into effect the different objects contained

the Government of Nepal for all practical purposes was Maharajah Jung Bahadur. Eleven years before (in 1846) Nepal was in a deplorable condition. In the Himalayan Kingdom, as elsewhere in oriental countries where women occupy an inferior place in the social order, equally with occidental lands where women are more or less on an equality with men, 'the sex' plays a great part. There has never been a revolution in Nepal—and revolutions have been many in that country—in which feminine influence has not been powerful; in some instances it has been predominant. So was it in 1846. Owing to the intrigues of the junior Queen of Maharajah Rajendro Bikram Shah,

---

in this treaty, and of promoting other verbal negotiations, the Governor-General and the Rajah of Nepal, under the impulse of their will and pleasure, depute a confidential person to each other, as Vakeel, that, remaining in attendance upon their respective Governments, they may effect the objects above specified, and promote whatever may tend to the daily improvement of the friendship subsisting between the two States.

ARTICLE XI.

It is incumbent upon the principals and officers of the two States, that they should manifest the regard and respect to the Vakeel of each other's Government, which is due to their rank, and is prescribed by the laws of nations; and that they should endeavour, to the utmost of their power, to advance any object which they may propose, and to promote their ease, comfort, and satisfaction, by extending protection to them, which circumstances are calculated to improve the friendship subsisting between the two Governments, and to illustrate the good name of both States throughout the universe.

ARTICLE XII.

It is incumbent upon the Vakeels of both States that they should hold no intercourse whatever with any of the subjects or inhabitants of the country, excepting with the officers of Government, without the permission of those officers; neither should they carry on any correspondence with any of them; and if they should receive any letter or writing from any such people, they should not answer it without the knowledge of the head of the State, and acquainting him of the particulars, which will

and the weakness of the Prime Minister, Futteh Jung Shah Chauthariah, complete disorder reigned in Nepal. It was successfully put an end to by Jung Bahadur when, acting under royal orders, he overthrew the malcontents, himself became Prime Minister, and gave to Nepal its first Constitution. The country, previously torn by faction and the deadly rivalries of the Chauthariahs, the Pandays, the Thapas, and the Bosinaths, now enjoyed peace and tranquillity. Unfortunately — but quite in accordance with Nepalese precedents — this result was not achieved without bloodshed; Jung Bahadur was altogether helpless in the matter, as what he did was done not only in self-defence, but in execution of his sovereign's commands, to have disobeyed which would have ensured certain death to himself.

In 1856, tired, as he declared, of office, Jung Bahadur resigned the Prime Ministership which he had held for ten years. He was soon induced to take the position once more, the office having been enhanced in importance with many splendid accessories, and at-

---

dispel all apprehension or doubt between us, and manifest the sincerity of our friendship.

ARTICLE XIII.

It is incumbent upon the principals and officers mutually to abide by the spirit of this treaty, which is now drawn out according to their faith and religion, and, deeming it in force from generation to generation, that they should not deviate from it; and any person who may transgress against it will be punished by Almighty God, both in this world and in a future state.

[A true translation]

(Signed), C. RUSSEL,

Assistant Persian Translator.

Ratified by the Governor-General and Council, 30th October, 1801, and by the Nepal Durbar on the 28th October, 1802.

tached for all time to Jung Bahadur and his family. The king conferred upon him and his heirs the title of Maharajah, and publicly invested him with the sovereignty of two provinces. He was given power of life and death, not only in regard to the two provinces granted to him, but also throughout Nepal. The Prime Minister's position was made hereditary, the succession being invested in Jung Bahadur's own brothers, one after another, and then in their sons, on a principle definitely laid down. This was not all. So far as foreign affairs were concerned Jung Bahadur was King and Government combined. In writing under the King's seal he was authorised 'to coerce the reigning King and his Minister, should they, according to his ideas, mismanage or endanger the relations between Nepal and the British Government, or between Nepal and the Chinese Government, or fail to act upon the advice which he might, under the circumstances, tender to them'.[1] In a word he was, constitutionally, made Dictator of his country in respect to foreign affairs. Obviously, in such a crisis as our Indian Empire passed through in 1857, his friendship or enmity was of importance to us. The conduct of Nepal towards the British Government was wholly in his keeping.

There was never much doubt that Jung Bahadur would discountenance the rebel movement in India, and throw the weight of his influence on the side of the British Government. With the Nana Sahib he had no sympathy (though refuge in Nepal was subsequently granted to a sister of the Nana); and, as to the success

[1] 'Sketches of Nepal', vol. ii, p. 17.

of the rebellion, he did not for a moment believe in its possibility. Colonel Ramsay, the Resident at Nepal, in a letter to Sir John Login,[1] expresses the belief that Jung Bahadur would have taken part against the Indian Government, if it had not been for what the Resident calls 'that providential visit of his to England, and the experience he gained there'. The visit, it may be added, was taken largely on the recommendation of the Residency Surgeon, Dr. Login, who had great influence with the Prime Minister of Nepal, and was to have taken charge of the Mission; unfortunately he died of cholera before the party started.

Strong pressure was brought to bear upon Jung Bahadur to side with the rebels. 'One of his brothers told me', says Colonel Ramsay, 'that every attempt was being made by influential men to induce him to join them in driving us out of the country, but that no persuasion would induce him to commit such an act of suicidal folly.' These attempts were renewed when the Nepalese General was in British India fighting Britain's battles. Against all such solicitation he stood firm. His loyal devotion to the British raj was proof against the most powerful temptations. Travel, and intimate acquaintance with his powerful neighbour, had had a useful and lasting effect upon him. As has been remarked, he had visited England, had been influenced by the might and power of Britain, especially as revealed in the wealth and populousness of London. As he him-

[1] 'Sir John Login and Duleep Sing' (W. H. Allen and Co., 1889), p. 456.

self was wont to remark, he had stood by London Bridge, had taken note of the ships on the river and the unending tide of life which flowed backwards and forwards across the bridge, and was enabled to form an estimate of the power and resources of the United Kingdom.[1]

The historian of the Mutiny makes emphatic reference to the influence of Jung Bahadur's visit to

---

[1] From the *Annual Register* for 1850 the following particulars of the visit to England are taken:—'*May*, 1850. The Nepalese Embassy landed at Southampton with all the *éclat* due to the political and personal distinction of its members. General Jung Bahadur Kumar Ranaju, the Prime Minister of Nepal, is described as being very handsome, and dark, with long jet black hair; he is but 32 years old, though already a distinguished warrior, and the most influential statesman in all Northern Hindustan. He was received by the Governor-General of India at Calcutta in full Durbar, and was saluted with nineteen guns on arriving and departing. He bears a complimentary letter to the Queen, and presents of surpassing costliness—worth a quarter of a million sterling. He is accompanied by his two brothers, who bear the title of colonel, six officers, and a suite of twelve servants. The first reception of these illustrious foreigners in this country was unfortunate—the Custom House officers insisted on searching the baggage. To this the noble Hindu felt a religious scruple; he is the first Brahmin of high caste who has come to Europe, and the infidel touch of the official would be religious pollution, difficult, and in some instances impossible, to expurge but by incremation of the article. He, therefore, intimated that, if any of his luggage or any of his suite were touched, he would not land on our shores, but would return to his country by the next steamer, without accomplishing the object of his mission; and he set a Hindu guard, with a drawn sword, to watch his luggage. After the "greatest alarm", and some interchange of telegraphic messages, the blunder was rectified; an order was given to pass the packages, and the Embassy landed, with property and honour alike intact.

'These distinguished guests became fashionable "lions" of the season—the handsome features and heroic bearing of the General (he has cut off some thirty heads with his own hands, and supplanted a rival ministry by shooting them in the presence of the Sovereign) made him the "admired of all observers". The General and his suite glittered with the most splendid jewels and gold. They were superbly armed, and scattered around gold and jewels with oriental profuseness. They

Europe upon his actions. 'The independent position occupied by Nepal', he says,[1] 'the known ability of the man, who, though only Prime Minister, wielded all real authority in the country, the certainty that the overthrow of the British could scarcely fail to offer great opportunities to an able General commanding a compact and well-disciplined army, gave to Jung Bahadur's proposal[2] the appearance of being inspired by a pure and generous friendship. Few untravelled independent rulers would have acted in a similar manner. But Jung Bahadur had but a few years previously visited Europe. The visit had enlightened him on many points, and one point in particular. It had convinced him that, under all circumstances, England would be able to maintain her hold on India.'

Not merely the might, but the mercy also, of England, impressed itself upon Jung Bahadur's mind. After his return from England—even though ten days after his arrival at Khatmandu a conspiracy was formed against him, and his death was intended—executions in Nepal became comparatively rare. Blood-shedding was disapproved of and avoided as much as possible. Writing a few years after Sir Jung Bahadur's death, and while his brother, Sir Ranadip Sing, was Prime Minister, the Residency doctor, from whose graphic and veracious pages extracts have already been made, says :—'Capital

---

were of course very liberally treated with dinners, reviews, and sights. Every means were taken to impress the minds of the Embassy with the wealth and grandeur of this country, and with such an exalted notion of our power as may convince the restless Nepalese (our nearest neighbours in Bengal) of the wisdom and policy of keeping on friendly terms.'

[1] Vol. iv, p. 221.

[2] To be described shortly.

punishments are now confined to cases of murder and culpable homicide. Jung has greatly mitigated the severity of the criminal code; and has altogether done away with "mutilation" as a punishment. The only case of mutilation of which I have heard since Jung's return occurred in 1852, and was richly deserved. A man went about the country giving out that Jung was intending to sacrifice one hundred and fifty infants as a propitiation to the deities, and that he (the prisoner) was commissioned by Jung to select the victims. Of course this produced a great sensation in the rural districts through which the man went, and mothers hastened to offer him large sums as bribes for him to pass their children and take others. The man was arrested, a grand parade assembled on the Tunakhal, the culprit's offence explained to the troops, and his tongue (the offending organ) cut out before them. He was then, minus his tongue, led away through all the districts where he had previously been, as a warning to show the people not only the falsity of his previous statements, but the consequences of so gross and wicked a lie against the powers that be.' English surroundings had such influence upon Jung Bahadur that he even discouraged the practice of suttee. In October, 1852, when Jung's most intimate friend, who had been with him from infancy and accompanied him to England ('Bana Captain Sahib') died, Jung, by his efforts and persuasions, succeeded in preventing either of his widows from performing suttee. 'He says, and probably truly, that when the common people get accustomed to see men of rank die and their bodies are burnt without suttee, they will, of their own accord, gradually give up such an inhuman and unreasonable practice.' Suttees still take place, but very rarely.

Under the circumstances described, Jung Bahadur acted in 1857 as might have been expected. He determined, immediately the news of the outbreak reached Khatmandu, to offer his assistance to the Indian Government. The position in which the British authorities were placed at this juncture, making co-operation on the part of the Nepalese Minister of special value, is set out in some detail in the sixth chapter of the fourth volume of Kaye and Malleson's 'Mutiny'. Oudh and Rohilkhand remained in open revolt: 'the dealing with them was to constitute the fourth scene of the drama.' Colonel Malleson, who so lucidly describes the situation in which the Indian Government was placed, tells, in a striking manner, the story of Nepalese help and Nepalese courage, how the one was rendered and the other displayed.

'It was the opinion of Sir Colin Campbell that the three months of cold weather which yet remained to him might be most profitably employed by following the enemy into Rohilkhand. By stamping out the rebellion in that province he would, he believed, assure the more easily the submission of the whole of the north-west. The separate forces then operating, as will be hereafter described, in western and central India, in Rájpútáná and in Bundelkhand, would at the same time restore order and tranquillity throughout those parts of India. Oudh alone would remain: and Sir Colin was of opinion that Oudh, hemmed in by the Gurkhas in one extremity, and by troops whom he would dispose in summer quarters from that extremity to the further border, might wait his pleasure—might remain, that is to say, for some months longer in the hands of the rebels, until the ensuing cold season would permit his troops to operate more effectually in that country. Rightly regarding his European troops as the mainstay—the backbone of his army, he was unwilling, if it could be avoided, to expose them to the exhaustion and loss inseparable from a hot-weather campaign—a campaign carried on under circumstances which would often require the employment of small detachments, hurried and forced marches, exposure to the mid-day sun, and possibly to the heavy autumnal rains.

'But, in the opinion of the Council of the Government of India, the political exigencies of the time were so pressing, that they overbore considerations which, if prompted partly by sound rules of military science, were dictated in the main by regard for the health and preservation of the European soldier. Lord Canning and the members of his Council were guided in the views they propounded by two great principles: the one, that no rest should be given to the rebels—that they must be attacked and pursued until they should submit; the other, that the main object of the next movement should be the re-capture of Lakhnao. These were cardinal points with the Government. Fitting in with them, too, was another consideration, which, if of a less pressing character, was yet not unimportant. I allude to the co-operation of the Gurkhas, led by the Prime Minister of Nepal, Jung Bahadur. These troops, ten thousand in number, were occupying a position from which they could co-operate effectively with the British in Oudh. Were Sir Colin to deal immediately with Oudh, they would join in the action. But it could not be expected, if the Oudh campaign were adjourned, that these men, natives of the Himalayas, would remain during the hot and rainy seasons in the plains exposed to a climate with which they were naturally unfitted to cope.

'There are few, I think, who would be disposed now to question the wisdom of the course recommended by the Government of India. It seems to me that every consideration favoured its adoption. Alike in war and politics, it is always advisable to strike a decisive blow at the most important of the exposed points of an enemy. In this case Lakhnao was that point. Lakhnao taken, the heart of the rebels would be broken. No other great rallying-place would remain to them. So long, on the other hand, as that regal city should remain in their possession, their adherents would continue to nourish hope, and it would require more than ordinary tact and care to prevent the renewal of uprisings in parts which had been already overrun.

'Again, of the two provinces, Rohilkhand and Oudh, the latter was by far the most formidable, the most important. The pacification of Rohilkhand would produce little or no effect on the men of Oudh. On the contrary, the re-conquest of Lakhnao would be felt in every village and in every corner of Rohilkhand. To this must be added the important consideration that whilst Outram was, with some difficulty, holding the Alambagh with nearly four thousand men, rebels from all parts of India were daily crowding into Lakhnao. This fact alone would show that the case of Lakhnao was the more pressing.

'The necessity of dealing in the first instance a

deadly blow at Lakhnao was insisted upon with so much force by Lord Canning that it became a law to the Commander-in-Chief. It devolved, then, upon him to make his preparations to carry into effect the settled plan.' . . .

'Among the offers of assistance which, in the early days of the revolt, had been made to the Governor-General, was one of peculiar significance. Jung Bahadur, the virtual ruler of the independent Hill State which, touching the British territory of Kumaun, extends all along the north-east border of Oudh, then rejoining British territory at a point in the Gorakhpur district due north of the station of that name, continues the touch to within a few miles of Darjeeling—Jung Bahadur, in the month of May, placed the whole military resources of Nepal at the disposal of the Governor-General. . . . . Lord Canning thanked Jung Bahadur for his offer, but it was not till the month of June that he accepted it. In pursuance of the agreement between the contracting parties, Jung Bahadur despatched three thousand Gurkhas from Khatmandu. These, entering the British territory at a point north of Gorakpur, marched on that place, and reached it at the end of the month. Their arrival was the signal for the disarming of the Sipáhis stationed there. The neighbouring stations of Azimgurh and Jaunpur were then in the throes of anarchy. Vainly had the heroic Venables, the indigo-planter, who had been steadfast among the faint-hearted, struggled and fought for order. It is true that on the 16th July, after a gallant fight of the few against many, he had repulsed the rebels in an attack on Azimgarh. But after the victory, his own followers had shown symptoms of mutiny, and he and the few Europeans who followed him had been forced, on the 30th July, to retreat on Ghazipore. To restore order, then, in Azimgarh and its vicinity, the arrival of tho Nepalese troops was opportune. They occupied Azimgarh on the 13th August, and Jaunpore on the 15th. Meanwhile, on their evaeuating it, Gorakhpore was taken possession of by rebels from Oudh, eommanded by one Mohammed Husen.

'The Government of India, to ensure concert between these allies and its own troops had transmitted orders to the military authorities at Benares to appoint eertain officers, left unemployed by the mutiny of their regiments, to join and aet with the Nepalese. In obedienee to these orders, Captain Boileau and Lieutenants Miles, Hall, and Campbell eame to Jaunpore and took up the duties assigned to them. Two or three weeks elapsed before an opportunity offered of testing the quality of the allied troops, but in the third week of September the approach to Azimgarh of a large body of rebels gave an occasion of which they eagerly availed themselves.

'Azimgarh was the point threatened. Lieutenant-Colonel Wroughton, commanding at Jaunpore, deemed it advisable then to detaeh the Shér regiment of Nepalese, twelve hundred strong, and two guns, to reinforce that station.

'The Nepalese left Jaunpore at 10 a.m. on the 18th September, marched forty miles that day, and reached Azimgarh at 6 o'elock in the evening. It had transpired, meanwhile, that the rebels were encamped at a village called Manduri, ten miles distant, and it being surmised that they were ignorant of the arrival of the Nepal reinforcement, it was determined to surprise them. Accordingly, at half-past one o'clock the next morning, the Shér regiment again set out, accompanied by Captain Boileau as English officer in charge of the force, by Mr. Wynand, the judge, by Mr. Venables, the gallant planter, and by three other officers. Manduri was reached a little after sunrise. The rebels were found strongly posted, their centre covered by the village, and their flanks protected by fields of sugar-cane, then at their full height. Nothing daunted, the Nepal colonel, Shamshere Sing, formed his men up in five columns, and dashed at that strong position. Their onslaught was so fierce, that in ten minutes the rebels were in full flight, leaving on the field three brass guns. They lost about two hundred men killed and wounded. On the side of the Nepalese two were killed and twenty-six wounded. Mr. Wynyard, in his report of the action to his civil superiors, alluded in the highest terms to the conduct of the Nepalese troops. . . . .

'This victory had an excellent effect. Up to that time the British authorities had felt some hesitation in employing their allies against the rebels, but with the victory of Manduri all uncertainty vanished. To march fifty miles in two days, and then to win a battle in an unknown country, would have reflected credit on veteran soldiers. The success obtained on this occasion not only filled the English officers with confidence, it emboldened them to follow up the step already taken. On the 27th September Colonel Wroughton, accompanied by the civil officers of the district, marched with another party of the Nepal troops from Jaunpore against, and occupied, Muharahpore, the stronghold of a rebel Rajah, Iradat Khan; took that chieftain prisoner; tried, and hanged him. Proceeding onwards, Wroughton and the Nepal troops pacified the entire district. On the 29th the authorities at Azimgarh made a similar demonstration before the place, and with similar success. Atraolia, the stronghold of the rebel leader Beni Madhu, was occupied, and its fortifications were destroyed. Up to the borders of Oudh order was thus for the time restored.

'To support the Nepal troops, the Government had, in September, directed the despatch from Benares of a small force, consisting of three hundred and twenty men of the 10th Foot, two nine-pounder guns, a small detachment of European artillery, and a hundred and seventy of the 17th Madras Native Infantry, under the command of Lieutenant-Colonel Longden of the 10th Foot. But, before this force could reach the scene of action, the Oudh rebels had again crossed the frontier, and had encountered and been beaten by the Nepalese at Kudya on the 19th October, and at Chanda on the 30th of the same month. The last-named action was severe enough to merit a separate record. The rebels mustered from four to five thousand strong, were strongly posted and had seven guns. The Nepal troops counted only eleven hundred men with two guns. The battle, obstinately contested, terminated in the complete defeat of the rebels, with a loss on their side of three hundred killed. Four of their guns were taken. But the victory was dearly purchased.

Lieutenant-Colonel Madan Man Sing and eleven men were killed, and fifty-nine were wounded. The gallantry of the Nepal troops had been conspicuous. Of one of them, Lieutenant Gamblin Sing, it is related in the official account of the action that, "single-handed, he took a gun, cutting down five of the artillery men, and wounding and driving away two others". This gallant ally was covered with wounds, but eventually recovered.

'Longden reached Jaunpore just after the action of Chanda. Three days after his arrival (4th November) the Oudh rebels, to the number of one thousand, with two guns, again crossed the Oudh frontier, and seized the fort of Atraolia. The attention of Longden was at once called to the fact. Uniting his force to that of the Nepalese, he marched out at once, and, on the ninth, cannonaded the place so vigorously that the enemy evacuated it during the night.

'But the fact that the British territory was still liable to invasion, and that the British troops, though strong enough to repel an isolated attack, were not strong enough to defend the whole frontier, and might be forced, under certain circumstances, to fall back on Benares, induced the Government of India to conclude with the Nepal Government a new arrangement. In virtue of this it was arranged that Jung Bahadur should proceed himself to the scene of action with a force of nine thousand picked troops, and that to this force Colonel MacGregor should be attached with the rank of Brigadier-General. At the same time measures were taken greatly to increase the British force on the eastern frontier of Oudh. Large reinforcements were sent to the Jaunpore force, and that force, so strengthened, was placed under the command of one of the ablest officers in the British army, Brigadier-General Franks, C.B. Similarly, another mixed force was organised in Western Behar by Colonel Rowcroft to move from Tirhoot along the Gandak towards Gorakhpore. These three *corps d' ármée* had but one primary object — to clear the British districts to the north of Benares and east of Oudh; as soon as these districts should be cleared, one corps would remain in observation, whilst the other two would march to co-operate with Sir Colin Campbell in his attack on Lucknow. It will be necessary then to deal with the three separately.

'Rowcroft's force was composed of thirty men of the Royal Marines, a hundred and thirty of the "Pearl" Naval Brigade under Sotheby, three hundred and fifty Nepal troops, fifty men of the Bengal Police Battalion, and four twelve-pounder howitzers, two of which were mountain train guns. It occupied an entrenched camp at Miurá, about forty-nine miles from Chapia. Seven miles distant, at Sohanpur, on the west bank of the little Gandak, lay a small rebel army, computed to consist of twelve hundred regular Sipáhis, and four thousand armed adventurers, of whom a hundred were mounted, with four guns. On the morning of the 26th December Rowcroft, who had waited for the arrival of the Gorákhnáth Nepal regiment from Segowli, marched to attack the rebel force. Their position was strong on two out of its three objective points. They occupied a village, covered in front by a tank with high banks, and on the right by a tope of trees; the left was comparatively uncovered. Rowcroft halted within half-a-mile of the place and rode forward to reconnoitre. He resolved to render useless the enemy's strong positions in the centre and on the right by turning his left. He did this with great coolness and success. The Nepal troops behaved splendidly under fire. Sotheby, of the Naval Brigade, managed the artillery with great skill. The Minié rifles of the Royal Marines, directed by Lieutenant Pym, produced a striking effect. The result was that the enemy, attacked a little after ten o'clock, were completely beaten by half-past one, forced back from Sohanpur, and followed six miles further to Majauli, and thence driven across the Gandak, with the loss of one large iron gun. Rowcroft followed up his victory the next day by crossing the river and destroying the homesteads of the leading rebels. Then, in pursuance of instructions he had received from Brigadier-General MacGregor, under whose orders he had been placed, he marched to Burhat Ghat on the river Ghághrá, there to await further instructions.

'Jung Bahadur's little army, meanwhile, setting out from Nepal had crossed the British frontier. On the 23rd of December it reached Battiah, eighty-two miles east of Gorakhpore. Here it was joined by MacGregor. Continuing its march, it crossed the river Gandak on the 30th, and arrived in the vicinity of Gorakhpore on the 5th of January. Gorakhpore was occupied by the rebels, but by rebels disheartened, divided in purpose, and hopeless of success. When attacked, then, the following morning by the Nepal army, they made but a feeble resistance, but fled across the

Rapti,[1] leaving seven guns in the possession of the conquerors. These lost but two men killed. Seven were wounded. The loss of the rebels amounted to about two hundred.

'The Civil Administration was at once re-established in Gorakhpore. The British districts were cleared of rebels. At the same time, awaiting the time when the Nepal force at Azimgarh should cross the Oudh frontier in co-operation with that under General Franks, MacGregor transmitted orders to Rowcroft to embark his little force in boats, and ascend the river.

'Before Rowcroft came up, the moment referred to had arrived, and Jung Bahadur, starting from Gorakhpore on the 14th of February, reached Barari, on the left bank of the Ghághrá, on the 19th. On the evening of that day Rowcroft anchored within four miles of that place, and landed on the right bank. There, on the morning of the 21st, he was joined by a brigade of the Nepal force, with six guns. Rowcroft then received orders to bring up his boats to Phulpur, so as to allow of their being used for the passage of the remainder of the Nepal force at that place. But before he could carry out this order, information reached Rowcroft that Phulpur was occupied by the rebels. Accordingly he marched on that place, drove the rebels from it, and captured three of their guns. Then, bringing up his boats, he made of them a bridge spanning the stream, and allowed

[1] The Rapti takes its rise in the sub-Himalayan ranges of Nepal, and, flowing round a long spur of mountains, enters the plains of Oudh, which it traverses in a south-easterly direction for ninety miles, passing through the Bahraich and Gondah districts; it finally joins the Ghághrá after a course of four hundred miles.

the Nepal troops to cross. It was then arranged that Rowcroft, with the "Pearl" Brigade, the Yeomanry Cavalry, which had joined him, and two Nepal regiments, should occupy Gorakhpore, to keep open the communications, whilst Jung Bahadur should march, via Sultanpur, on Lakhnao.

'Crossing the Ghághrá, Jung Bahadur marched to Ambarpur on the 25th February. The road to that place was commanded by a small fort, having a triple line of defence within a bamboo jungle, and defended by thirty-four men. It was necessary to storm this post, for, though it might be turned, its continued occupation by the rebels would enable them to act on the communications of the advancing force. The Nepal troops then were sent against it. It was defended with so much vigour and resolution, that the assailants lost seven men killed and forty-three wounded before they gained possession of it. The defenders died, all, at their posts.

'The effect of this capture was great, for two days later the rebels evacuated a large fort occupied by two hundred men, towards which the Nepalese were advancing. Neither their passage across the Gamti near Sultanpur, nor their further progress to Lakhnao, was disturbed by the enemy. They reached the vicinity of that city on the 10th of March, and moved into line with the British army on the 11th, in full time to take part in the capture of that city.

'I purpose now to turn to General Franks. On the 29th November that officer had been appointed to command the troops in the Azimgarh and Jaunpore districts. The force at his disposal consisted of about five thousand five hundred men — of whom three thousand two hundred were Nepalese — and twenty guns.' After describing various exploits of the General, leading up to the joining of the Nepalese troops with his command, the historian continues: 'He joined Sir Colin Campbell on the night of the 4th March, having, in thirteen days, marched a hundred and thirty miles, beaten an enemy immensely superior in four general actions, and captured thirty-four pieces of ordnance, with the small loss of thirty-seven officers and men killed and wounded."[1]

On the 11th of March, the Nepal troops, led by the Maharajah Jung Bahadur, were brought into line. This reinforcement enabled Sir Colin Campbell to extend his plan of operations on the succeeding days. The next day the Nepal troops were ordered to advance on the British left, so as to hold the line of the canal. This operation drew the attention of a portion of the rebel force to that quarter. Colonel Malleson, dealing with the events of the 14th of March, says:—'Two days previously, the Commander-in-Chief (Sir Colin Campbell) had requested Jung Bahadur and the Nepalese to move to his left, up the canal, and take in reverse the positions which, for three months, the rebels had occupied in front of the Alambágh, the garrison of which was now reduced to two regiments. Jung Bahadur carried out the instructions conveyed to him with ability and success. One after another the enemy's positions, from the Chár-bágh Bridge up to the Residency, with their guns, fell into his hands. This operation, which

[1] 'History of the Sepoy Mutiny of 1857–8,' iv., c. 7, p. 221, *et seq.*

effectually covered, as it was carried out, the Commander-in-Chief's left, occupied several days. The losses the Nepal Chief experienced were inconsiderable.'

In a footnote Colonel Malleson writes: 'Jung Bahadur's successful advance was memorable for the recovery from captivity of two English ladies—Miss Jackson and Mrs. Orr. In the third volume of this history (note, p. 252-6) I have given a sketch of the adventures of the Sitapur fugitives, and have told how it was that on the 17th March only two of them, Mrs. Orr and Miss Jackson, survived. On the 20th March two British officers attached to the Nepal troops, Captain McNeill and Lieutenant Boyle, when exploring some deserted streets near the Kaiserbagh, were informed by a friendly native of the place in which the two ladies were confined. They at once procured the aid of a party of fifty Nepalese, and after walking through narrow streets — about half-a-mile — they reached a house occupied by one Wajid Ali, an officer of the Old Court. In a room within the house they found the two ladies, dressed in Oriental costume. They at once procured a palanquin, and notwithstanding the opposition threatened by a body of ruffians, who would have prevented the rescue, they conveyed the ladies in safety to the camp of Jung Bahadur.'

In another direction also the Nepalese troops rendered aid. Describing the services of Mr. George Yule in Eastern Behar, the historian makes the following references to movements in which Nepalese soldiers took part:—

'Yule, I have said, had, by his prompt and vigorous

movements, saved the British districts on the right bank of the Kusi from invasion, and forced the rebels to seek refuge in Nepal territory. There, at a place thirty-six miles from the British frontier, they were detained by the Nepalese authorities, pending instructions from Jung Bahadur. It was useless for Yule to wait any longer on the frontier, or to disquiet himself regarding the fate of men no longer able to plunder and destroy. . . . .

'Richardson joined Yule on the 11th January. The rebels were still at Chatra. Just about the same time the practical reply of Jung Bahadur to Yule's representations regarding the mutineers of the 11th Irregulars was received. That reply took the shape of an order to his lieutenant on the spot, Ratan Man Singh, to attack the mutineers, in co-operation with the English. It unfortunately happened that the force at the disposal of Ratàn Man Singh consisted mostly of untrained infantry militia, and only a few trained artillerymen with their guns. The Nepalese commander was therefore unwilling to assent to any manœuvre which would necessitate division of his own force. After some discussion, then, it was agreed between himself on the one side, and Mr. Yule and Major Richardson on the other, that whilst the Nepal troops should guard the roads leading eastward, and Richardson with his cavalry should watch the right bank of the Kusi, Yule's infantry should attack Chatra. Yule and Richardson were aware that it would have been far better that the Nepal commander should watch the left as well as the right bank of the river, for the upper part of the left bank could not, from the nature of the country, be effectually guarded by cavalry. But, under the circumstances, it was the best thing to be done, and, after all, they both believed that the rebels would fight. To give time to the Nepal commander to make his arrangements, the 21st was fixed upon as the day for the attack.

'This delay proved fatal to the success of the plan. Yule crossed the Nepal frontier on the 14th, and on the 19th reached Pirara, about ten miles from Chatra. Richardson meanwhile had advanced to Chauria, a place which commanded the only path by which he believed the mutineers could possibly proceed westward, should they cross the river above it. But whether the mutineers had been warned, or whether they gained information from their scouts, it is certain that as soon as they heard that Yule had reached Pirara, they crossed the river, and marched westward. Yule and Richardson pushed after them; but, as it was seen that the rebels were following a line of country totally impracticable for cavalry, Richardson proceeded by rapid marches to Darbangah to cover Tirhoot, whilst Yule returned to his division—which was not subsequently disturbed. The mutineers succeeded in making their way into north-eastern Oudh, only eventually to fall by the bullet and the sword.'

Of the return of the Nepalese soldiery to their own country, the rebels having been everywhere defeated and nearly all dispersed, the particulars which follow are given :—

'Bitauli evacuated, Hope Grant proceeded to look after Jung Bahadur's Nepalese. He found them at Masauli, midway between Ramnagar and Nawabganj. In his journal, the General gives a vivid description of the condition of our allies. "The European officer in command," he writes, "had great difficulties to contend with in marching through a country so filled with rebels. His force consisted of eight thousand men with twenty guns, yet he could only reckon on two thousand men for actual fighting purposes. He had two thousand sick and four thousand carts; and each of the latter being filled with tents, private property, and loot, required, according to the usages of these troops, a man to guard it." As these troops took no further part in the war, it may be convenient to state here that they continued their retreat from Masauli towards their own country, and effected it without molestation. They reached Gorakhpore early in May, and resumed their march thence on the 17th *idem.* In consequence of the number of their carts they experienced some difficulty in crossing the Gandak at Bagaha, in the Champaran district. Marching thence by way of Bhatia and Sigauli, they crossed the Nepal frontier early in June.'

Such services as these, proffered in so handsome a manner, performed with such gallantry and success, show in what manner Jung Bahadur understood Art. III of the Treaty of 1801, and the opinion he cherished of what constituted friendship between States. The manner in which the Government of India to-day interpret their duty to the daughter of Jung Bahadür and to other relatives of his, who are now refugees in India, will appear in sufficient detail—too sufficient for any one who cherishes pride in the British name. In the comparison the Christian rulers of India do not shine: they are shamed by the greater nobleness of the non-Christian Himalayan Highlander. This is a calamity. England in India cannot afford to be outdone in generosity and nobleness of conduct by any Asiatic, however eminent, unless the bases of our rule of the great Empire of India are to be altered. For the Indian Government to be put to shame in generous conduct and righteous behaviour is not a calamity merely; it is a serious danger. To be taught its duty by an Asiatic Prince, however brave and distinguished, is for the Indian authorities themselves to undermine the structure on which our rule is established, and to make that rule itself insecure.

CHAPTER III.

APPRECIATING THE SERVICES OF THE 'FRIEND IN NEED'.

Maharajah Jung Bahadur's eminent services were not allowed by Lord Canning to go without recognition or reward. Lord Lyveden, in March, 1860, moved, in the House of Lords, for a return of the honours and rewards conferred upon Princes of India and others for services rendered during the Mutiny. A Blue Book was presented. The correspondence in it relating to Nepal is of special interest in connection with the tale that is told in these pages.

Brigadier-General MacGregor, the British Military Commissioner with the Nepalese force, placed on record the high sense he entertained of the value and extent of the services performed. 'Embracing with firmness the alliance of the British Government from the first,' said the Brigadier-General, 'his Highness Maharajah Jung Bahadur has never swerved in his loyalty. Assailed by temptations of all sorts, he has thrown them all aside, and at once acquainted me both with the agents and their promises. He has cheerfully endured privation and exposure himself, and expended the blood of his soldiers in the cause of justice and humanity, and in what he has the sagacity to perceive lie the best interests of his own State. He has led his troops in person in battle, and there they have shown the qualities which have made their nation famous.'

Not only did Lord Canning himself personally express acknowledgments to Jung Bahadur: he made him a Grand Cross of the Bath (Military Division) while a cession of territory was offered to the King of Nepal, Jung Bahadur being chosen as the medium through which the announcement of the cession should be conveyed. The Governor-General told the Nepalese warrior that 'the friendly condition of his Government, and the exertions and successes of his troops would be held in grateful recollection, not less in England than in India'. Nearly eighteen years later the Prince of Wales, when visiting Nepal, repeated Britain's obligations, and declared they should never be forgotten. At the present moment, in Calcutta, those services are regarded as if they had never been performed. Indeed, as the support given to certain Afghan enemies of the State has proved, active antagonism appears to be a surer road to the heart of the Government of India and a more potent instrument to call forth the friendly regard of its Foreign Office than the most devoted friendship and the greatest expenditure of blood and treasure in fighting its battles.

Earlier pages have contained the historian's record of Jung Bahadur's services. It may be well now to let the Governor-General of the day, in his despatches to the Secret Committee of the East India Company, to the King of Nepal, and to Jung Bahadur himself, tell the story of how Jung Bahadur's help was regarded by the head of the Indian Government thirty-two years ago.

The first of these documents is dated 30th May, 1858, is addressed to the Secret Committee in Leadenhall Street, and is in these terms :—

Honourable Sirs,

I have the honour to report to you the steps which I have taken to mark the appreciation by the British Government of the great services rendered to it by the army of Nepal under the command of his excellency, Jung Bahadur.

His Excellency long ago signified a wish, to which I gladly assented, that I should receive him, here or elsewhere, on his return from Oudh to Nepal; and at the close of the operations against Lucknow, he marched to Allahabad, accompanied by two regiments of infantry and a field battery.

His Excellency arrived here on the first of last month, and his camp was pitched within a mile of this house.

His Excellency was attended by some of the chief officers of his army, amongst whom were his brothers, Generals Ranadip Sing and Dhir Shumshere.

The usual visits of ceremony took place, and I had the satisfaction of offering to the Maharajah, in full Durbar, my cordial thanks for the aid which the Government of India had received from him, and from his brave soldiers, and my assurance that the friendly conduct of his Government, and the exertions and successes of his troops, would be held in grateful recollection, not less in England than in India.

Jung Bahadur was earnest in his declarations of attachment to the British Government, and took occasion to commend highly the services and conduct of General MacGregor, C.B., and of the other officers whom I had attached to his head-quarters.

He seemed desirous to impress upon me the inability of his hill-men to bear the heat of the plains at this season, and that this made him anxious for their return to Nepal as soon as possible.

On the 8th of April, the day before Jung Bahadur's departure from Allahabad, I received his Excellency at a private audience, at which only his own vakeel, who understands English, and the Secretary to Government in the Foreign Department, were present.

On this occasion, acting upon the discretionary authority

conveyed to me in your letter of the 9th February, I announced to his Excellency the intention of the British Government to offer to the Maharajah of Nepal the restitution of a portion of the territory which was ceded by Nepal in 1815, and my wish that his Excellency should be the channel through which the offer should be made to his Sovereign and to the Nepalese Durbar; it being made in recognition of great services rendered to British India by himself and by the troops which he commands.

I have the honour to enclose copies of letters which, on the 17th instant, I addressed to his Highness the Maharajah of Nepal, and to Maharajah Jung Bahadur.

Your honourable Committee will see that in the letter to the Maharajah of Nepal I have described the territory to be restored to Nepal as the whole of the former Gurkha possessions below the hills, extending from the River Gopa on the west to the British territory of Gorakpur on the east, and bounded on the south by Khyrugarb and the district of Baraitch, and on the north by the hills. This constitutes that portion of the territory ceded by Nepal in 1815, which in 1816 was made over by the British Government to the Nawab Vizier of Oudh, and in return for which, and for the cession of the district of Khyrughur, the Nawab Vizier cancelled a debt due by the British Government to himself of one million sterling.

It is a tract 200 miles long, of varying breadth, and adjoining the province of Oudh from end to end.

The other portions of the territory ceded by Nepal in 1815 adjoined our own old provinces, and have been from that time absorbed into them.

I propose that the new boundary line between the Nepalese territory and the British province of Oudh should be marked out in the cold season of this year. It will not be possible to enter upon this work, with due regard for the health of those employed, before the end of November.

To the King of Nepal, Lord Canning had, thirteen days previously, sent the following letter:

After compliments.

I addressed a letter to your Highness on the 23rd December

last, congratulating you on the achievements of a portion of your Highness's forces at Chanda and Koohona.

Since that time the main body of the auxiliary force of your Highness, under the immediate command of Maharajah Jung Bahadur, has been in co-operation with the British army, and has greatly distinguished itself.

The troops composing it have fought at Sahibgunje, at Peepraieh, at Gorakpur, at Shagrenje, at Phoolpur, at Jalalpur, and at Konda Nuddee, and they have in every instance been victorious.

Maharajah Jung Bahadur reached Lucknow in time to assist in the investment and capture of that city. The service which the Maharajah rendered was rendered with the greatest zeal and courage, and was very valuable.

I now desire to offer to your Highness the cordial thanks of the Government of India for the assistance thus given by the troops of Nepal. Within a few days of this time those troops will have recrossed the British frontier, and I wish that their return to your Highness's dominions should be marked, not only by this written expression of thanks, but by a public and substantial token of the estimation in which the British Government hold your Highness's friendly conduct.

To this end I have determined, on the part of the British Government, to restore to the Nepal State the whole of the former Gurkha possessions below the hills, extending from the river Gogna on the West, to the British territory of Gorakpur on the East, and bounded on the South by Khyrugarh and the district of Bareitch, and on the North by the hills. Measures will hereafter be taken at a favorable season of the year to mark out the exact boundaries, by means of commissioners to be appointed on the part of the British Government and the State of Nepal.

I trust that the return of this territory to your Highness's rule will be acceptable to your Highness and to the Nepalese Durbar.

I wish your Highness to be assured that the great services which have rendered by your brave soldiers and their distinguished leader, are appreciated by the British Government, and that the goodwill and friendship of England towards your country is sincere and lasting.

(sd.) CANNING.

On the same day, 17th May, 1858, the Governor-General wrote to Jung Bahadur as follows:—

Sir,

Your Excellency will remember that on the last occasion on which I had the pleasure of receiving your Excellency on the eve of your departure from Allahabad, I announced to you my intention to restore to the Maharajah of Nepal a certain tract of country adjoining the frontier of his kingdom, which had been ceded to the British Government in 1816. Your Excellency will also remember that I expressed a wish that you should be the medium of the communication to the Maharajah.

The restitution is made in recognition and as a lasting memorial of great services rendered by your Excellency in person and by the brave troops under your command to the British Government. It cannot, therefore, be made known to the Maharajah and to the Durbar through any channel so fitting as yourself.

The last of the regiments which composed your Excellency's army are now about to cross the British frontier on their return to Nepal.

I, therefore, again repeat to these gallant men, and to your Excellency as their leader, my cordial thanks for the good service which they have performed, and I place in your Excellency's hands the letter to the Maharajah communicating to his Highness the cession of the territory to which I have alluded.

Towards the close of the following year, that is in October, 1859, General Ramsay, the Resident at Khatmandu, described the investiture of Jung Bahadur with the insignia of the Bath in a letter to the Government of India.

'I have the honour,' he said, 'to acknowledge the receipt of your letter, No. 5707, of the 17th ultimo, and its accompaniments, conveying instructions for the delivery to Maharajah Jung Bahadur of the collar and badge appendant of a Knight Grand Cross, Military Division, of the Most Honourable Order of the Bath, and the investment badge and star,[1] also a copy of the statutes of the order, and a sealed packet containing Her Majesty's grant and warrant or dispensation of investiture, and a letter from His Royal Highness Prince Albert.

'2nd. All your instructions have been minutely carried out. The sealed packet was opened by the Maharajah, to whom I fully explained its contents; and his Excellency afterwards, in my presence, signed the engagement (herewith returned), promising to restore the collar and appendant badge in the event of his ceasing to be a member of the order, etc.[2]

'3rd. The representations of the insignia of the Bath, referred to in several parts of the statutes as being annexed to them, did not accompany them.

'4. I presented the insignia to his Excellency, as desired, on the 15th instant, at a full durbar; royal

---

[1] All received by Dawk Banghy.

[2] The document was as follows:—'I do hereby acknowledge to have received from the Lord Chamberlain of Her Majesty's household the collar and badge appendant of a Knight Grand Cross (Military Division) of the Most Honourable Order of the Bath; and I hereby covenant and promise, that in case I should hereafter cease to hold my rank and place as a member of the Order of the Bath, I will forthwith restore to the Registrar and Secretary the said collar and badge; and I further promise that I will, without delay, make due provision for the restoration of the said collar and badge by my personal representatives, in case I shall continue a member of the Order until the period of my decease.

'Witness my hand, this twenty-fourth day of September, one thousand eight hundred and fifty-nine.

'By MAHARAJAH JUNG BAHADUR RANAGER, Minister and Commander-in-Chief of Nepal.

'Signed in the presence of

'G. RAMSAY, Lieutenant-Colonel, Resident at the Court of Nepal, and of

'H. OLDFIELD, Honorary Assistant Resident.

'(Signed) G. RAMSAY, Resident.'

salutes were fired in honour of Her Majesty and of Prince Albert, when I put them into his hands, and every care was taken to render the ceremony as imposing as possible, in accordance with the Maharajah's own ideas, whose wishes I consulted before we arranged the details of the presentation.

'5th. Addresses, which, at Maharajah Jung Bahadur's suggestion, had been prepared in the Parbuthah language, were read to the assembled sirdars by the Raji Goras of the durbar, such being considered by his Excellency as the most public and at the same time the most complimentary manner in which they could be delivered, so as to be perfectly intelligible to his Highness the Maharajah Dheraj and to the members of his Court.

'6th. The Mahila Sahib, the king's brother, was present on the occasion, this being the first time, since his release from imprisonment, that I have ever met him at a public durbar.

'7th. After the ceremony Maharajah Jung Bahadur gave me a nuzzur of two gold Mohurs [these will be carried to public account], in token of his respect for Her Majesty Queen Victoria, and he afterwards presented me to the Maharajah Dheraj.

'8th. His Excellency appeared greatly pleased, and spoke in warm terms in acknowledgment of the high honor which has been conferred upon him; and both he and the Maharajah desired me to convey to the Viceroy and Governor-General their sincere reciprocation of his kind feelings, and their grateful thanks for the manner in which his lordship desired me to express them. He will address a letter in reply to the communication he has received from His Royal Highness Prince Albert, the Great Master of the Order of the Bath, in the course of a few days, which he trusts that the Governor-General will do him the favour to transmit to England.

'I have, etc.,
'(Signed) G. RAMSAY,
'Resident.'

As stated in the Resident's letter, Jung Bahadur expressed his intention of addressing a letter to Prince Albert. He did so. This was the communication:

'YOUR ROYAL HIGHNESS,—

'I have had the honour to receive your letter, dated Buckingham Palace, the 18th of April, 1859, announcing to me that Her Majesty the Queen of England has been graciously pleased to nominate and appoint me to be an honorary member of the Military Division of the First Class, or Knight Grand Cross of the Order of the Bath, of which your Royal Highness is the Great Master.

'I have also received Her Majesty's grant, and the warrant of dispensation with the ceremony of investiture, a copy of the statutes, and also the various insignia of the Order, which have been transmitted to me by his Excellency the Viceroy and Governor-General of India through Lieutenant-Colonel G. Ramsay, his lordship's representative at this court.

'I beg that your Royal Highness will be pleased to convey to Her Majesty my sincere acknowledgments for this very high mark of favour and of honour, and that you will also express the gratification I feel at the high consideration with which Her Majesty regards my humble services, which will again be freely placed at the Viceroy's disposal should occasion ever arise upon which they may be likely to be useful.

'I beg also to thank your Royal Highness for your congratulations, and the kind wishes you have expressed for my happiness and for the preservation of my health and life. I desire to return these compliments, both in my own and my sovereign's name. It is our united hope that all prosperity and happiness may continue to attend her most gracious Majesty and yourself, and that I may be permitted to subscribe myself as

'Your Royal Highness's sincere friend,

'SRI JUNG BAHADUR (L.S.).'

Afterwards, when the Most Exalted Order of the Star of India was founded, no name so readily suggested itself for the highest rank in that order—Knight Grand Commander—as that of Sir Jung Bahadur, G.C.B. As frontispiece to this volume will be found a likeness of Sir Jung Bahadur in his robes as Knight Grand Commander.[1]

In addition to all this, the praise of Sir Jung Bahadur was ever trickling from the Anglo-Indian journalist's pen into the columns of his newspaper. Indeed, so frequently were the Nepalese Minister's good deeds and friendship mentioned in public prints that, probably, no name became better known in India than did Jung Bahadur's. His family knew this. They

[1] This likeness and some of the others published in this work are from photographs taken by Messrs. Bourne and Shepherd, of Calcutta.

supposed that what the organs of public opinion in India uttered was sincere. They remembered, too, all that was said, many times over, by royal and influential personages of the indebtedness of the Empire to the Nepal Maharajah, and bore in mind that, so recently as the viceroyalty of Lord Northbrook, Sir Jung Bahadur was treated with special distinction on a visit to Calcutta. They reposed in full confidence upon the friendship of the Indian Government. That confidence was destined to a rude awakening.

CHAPTER IV.

SHAKSPERE'S 'MACBETH' IN NEPALESE ROYAL AND NOBLE LIFE.

Four years ago—that is, in November, 1885—an incident occurred which was destined to put the sincerity of the friendliness so frequently expressed by the Prince of Wales, as representing the Home Country, by the Government of India, and by the Indian newspapers, to the test. The tragedy which, occurring in Scotland, gave Shakspere the materials for his 'Macbeth,' was repeated in a valley in the Himalayan mountains. In Nepal, side by side with a slight veneer of the civilization of the nineteenth century, is to be found a condition of things which is closely comparable with the state of Scotland in the eleventh century. Personal ambitions on the part of powerful nobles and ancient families lead to incidents which, in almost every respect, are the counterparts of scenes in Scottish history. The narrative to be set out hereafter in some detail exactly follows the Caledonian precedent. Macbeth's inordinate ambition led him to murder Duncan, his kinsman and sovereign; and the crime was rendered deeper and blacker by the high honours which had been profusely showered upon him by his royal master immediately before the murder. It was exactly the same inordinate ambition that prompted Bir Shumshere, a nephew of Jung Bahadur, to accomplish the destruction of his uncle, the late Regent of Nepal, and in his case also the criminality of the offence has been immeasurably enhanced by the fact of his having been promoted to high command by the unsuspecting Minister shortly before the perpetration of the atrocious crime. In both cases there was a base return for kindnesses received, and an abuse of generous confidence which cannot fail to excite a thrill of horror in the human breast. Duncan's murder was falsely attributed to his sons, Malcolm and Donalbain; in like manner also have the murderers of Sir Ranadip Sing sought to fix the guilt of their enormity upon his son, Dhoje Nursing. And, just as Macbeth followed up the murder of Duncan with that of his rival Banquo, so Bir Shumshere followed up the murder of his uncle with that of his brave cousin, Juggut Jung. The subsequent massacres by Macbeth have also had their parallel in Nepal, and the Indian usurper, equally with his Scottish archetype, is

> 'Cabined, cribbed, confined, bound in
> To saucy doubts and fears—'

the effect of those compunctious visitings of conscience which, by the decrees of fate, attend all who are guilty of the crime of Cain.

> 'Now does he feel
> His secret murders sticking on his hands;
> Now minutely revolts upbraid his faith-breach;
> Those he commands move only in command,
> Nothing in love; now does he feel his title
> Hang loose about him, like a giant's robe
> Upon a dwarfish thief.'

Like Macbeth, Bir Shumshere has yet to reckon with those whom he has grievously wronged. Duncan's son took refuge in England; and the King of England, moved by sympathy with his great misfortune, lent him a force of ten thousand men to assist in the overthrow of the Scottish usurper. With this aid, Malcolm, son of the murdered Duncan, was happily able to destroy the usurper, and to recover the throne of his father. The son of the murdered Sir Ranadip Sing, and the daughter of Sir Jung Bahadur, are refugees in British territory.

There, unfortunately, the parallel ends. Although the claims of the kinsfolk of Sir Jung Bahadur are, by Treaty and by reason of service rendered in a time of serious calamity, incomparably greater than any of the royal Duncan's sons could have upon Edward the Confessor, the Government of India have wholly failed to show either personal kindness to the refugees, or even that bare justice which precedent[1] not merely justified but strongly impelled, while the interests of the country itself have been wholly ignored.

When Sir Jung Bahadur died in 1877, he was succeeded by his brother, Sir Ranadip Sing, K.C.S.I. The Premiership, was, in 1846, as has been already set forth, made an appanage of Jung Bahadur's family. The constitution then agreed to by the King provided that on the Prime Minister's death the next brother in

[1] On one occasion the Government of India actually advanced money out of British Indian revenues to a Nepalese refugee who, unlike these relatives of Sir Jung Bahadur, possessed no claim whatever upon the goodwill of the Government.

age should succeed him.[1] His two surviving brothers were Sir Ranadip Sing and Dhir Shumshere. The former, in due course, became Prime Minister, the latter Commander-in-Chief of the Nepalese army. Both brothers worked together with the utmost harmony, and the country had peace and great prosperity under their governance.

Sir Ranadip Sing fought for India during the Mutiny; he was second in command of the Nepalese contingent. He was as stedfast in his friendship to the British Government as was his great and illustrious brother himself. This he proved in a most significant manner. During the recent wars with Afghanistan he placed the military resources of Nepal at the disposal

---

[1] The several claimants to the Prime Ministership in order of precedence are the following:

1. Sir Ranadip Sing Bahadur—assassinated.

2. Jeet Jung 3. Puddum Jung 4. Ranabir Jung	} Sons of Sir Jung Bahadur.

5. Yudh Protap, grandson of Sir Jung Bahadur—murdered.
6. Kedar Nursing, nephew of Sir Jung Bahadur.
7. Bir Shumshere Jung, son of Dhir Shumshere (deceased brother of the late Sir Jung Bahadur), ringleader of the usurpers.
8. Amur Jung—exiled with family to Pokhra, a most unhealthy station.
9. Dhoje Nursing, only son of Sir Ranadip Sing.
10. Khurg Shumshere Jung.
11. Bhopendro Jung—exiled to Pokhra with family.

12. Run Shumshere Jung 13. Deb Shumshere Jung 14. Chundra Shumshere Jung 15. Bhim Shumshere Jung 16. Futteh Shumshere Jung 17. Lalit Shumshere Jung 18. Jut Shumshere Jung	} Sons of Bir Shumshere, and followers of their father.

19. Bhoyrub Nursing Bahadur—sent to the hills.
20. Icha Bikram, adherent of Bir Shumshere.

HIS EXCELLENCY MAHARAJAH SIR RANADIP SING RANA BAHADUR,
K.C.S.I., ETC., ETC., LATE PRIME MINISTER OF NEPAL.

of the Governor-General, thereby carrying out the friendly policy announced by Sir Jung Bahadur in his letter to the Prince Consort. 'I beg,' said Jung to Prince Albert, 'that you will be pleased to convey to her Majesty . . . . the gratification I feel at the high consideration with which her Majesty regards my humble services, which will again be placed at the Viceroy's disposal should occasion ever arise upon which they may be likely to be useful.' The significance of such an offer is unmistakable, especially in view of the powerful assistance which, it is now recognised, the semi-independent States of India can render to the Paramount Power. To all the help these States can give, the Indian Government may, if they choose, add the brave warriors of the Himalayan slopes. The offer of Sir Ranadip Sing at such a time was of vast importance. To Russia it meant that should an attack ever be made by her on India she would have to reckon not merely with the forces of the British Empire as contained in the Indian Army List, and in the Feudatory States, but also with the gallant mountaineers beyond the Indian North-Eastern frontier. Surely such friendship as this was worth cherishing. Having such a friend on our flank it might be supposed the Government of India would take care to bind that friend to itself with the indissoluble bonds of friendly regard. In 1857, and again in 1878, Sir Jung Bahadur's family gave unmistakeable evidence of *their* friendship to England and England's Empire in the East.

Lord Northbrook, while Viceroy, recognised Ranadip Sing's cordiality towards the rulers of India and his good services during his great brother's life-time. The

Nepalese noble was created a Knight Commander of the Star of India. Afterwards, when he had succeeded his brother, the enlightened character of his rule was recognised by the Chinese Government, which conferred upon him a very high title. As an administrator Sir Ranadip Sing was the author of many domestic reforms, the carrying out of which largely added to the material prosperity of Nepal. Some of these reforms may be instanced. The enumeration of them will indicate the high-minded principles on which the affairs of Nepal were conducted.

1. Reform of the land settlement. The system of farming the land revenue before his accession to power worked most grievous injury to the whole people; he altered this, and introduced the ryotwari settlement, giving the cultivating classes a real and permanent interest in their lands.

2. Financial reforms. He established for the first time an efficient system for the collection of the national revenues, and founded a system of audit of accounts. In former times the fiscal officers of the State were virtually irresponsible agents; they are now subject to a close system of supervision and scrutiny, and defalcations are hardly known.

3. The organization of a Public Works Department.

4. The establishment of banks for facilitating trade operations.

5. Reforms in the criminal law and in the administration thereof, the barbarous penalties prescribed in the old laws being superseded by a more rational system of primitive correction; and various measures adopted for ensuring justice to all.

6. Reclamation of waste lands; development of the tea industry; abolition of monopolies in *chirata*, mines, tobacco, and dry fish; abolition of poll tax levied on pilgrims; encouragement given to the cultivation of Sanscrit by the establishment of schools; establishment of hospitals and dispensaries for the sick poor; and development of local industries, special encouragement being given to every kind of mechanical skill.

'These are imperial works and worthy kings.'

CHAPTER V

A NEPHEW'S GRATITUDE AND HIS MANNER OF SHOWING IT.

After the defeat of the Liberal Party at the polls in 1874 the leader of the Party, Mr. Gladstone, partially retired from public life. In a letter to Lord Granville, written in January, 1875, he re-iterated his desire, expressed in March of the preceding year, to give up political work. He declared he saw no advantage in continuing to act as the leader of the Liberal party, and added: 'At the age of sixty-five, and after forty-two years of a laborious public life, I think myself entitled to retire at the present opportunity. This retirement is dictated to me by my personal views as to the best method of spending the closing years of my life.' On not a few other occasions the veteran statesman has expressed his desire to put public affairs in the background, and to devote the remainder of his days to retirement and contemplation upon those things which make for eternal peace. In this feature of his character Mr. Gladstone is in accord with the Hindu ideal and, so far as may be, the Hindu practice.

Professor Max Müller, in a learned article,[1] has

[1] *New Review*, December, 1889.

shown that, in olden days in India, life was divided into certain stations, or periods. The first was devoted to education—of the hand as well as of the head—and was the student life; the second was that of the householder, in which 'he had to perform all the duties of a husband and father, offer a number of obligatory and optional sacrifices, continue his study of the Veda, and, if a Brahmin, be ready to teach'; in the third stage, his children having grown up and having assumed family responsibilities, 'the householder ought to know that the time had come for leaving his house and all its cares, and retiring from the village into the forest,"[1] and finally, 'when at last life and all its interests ceased to have any attraction, when he lived already more in the next world than in this, then the time came, for the members of the first caste at least, to bid farewell to all, to leave the forest abode near the village, and to enter upon the final *Asrama*, that of *Samnyâssi*.'[2]

[1] 'This seems to us a great wrench, and a sacrifice difficult to bear. It could, however, hardly have been so in India. Life in the forest there was a kind of *villeggiatura*. Property being almost entirely family property, the father simply gave up to his sons what he himself no longer required. When he withdrew from the village, he became released from many duties. He was allowed to take his wife with him, and his friends and relations were allowed to see him in his sylvan retreat. He was then called a *Vânaprastha*, a dweller in the forest, and, released from the duties of a householder, from sacrificial and other ceremonial obligations, he was encouraged to meditate on the great problems of life, to rise above the outward forms of religion, and to free himself more and more from all the fetters which once bound him to this life.'

[2] '*Samnyâssi* means a man who has divested himself of everything, who is free from all fetters, not only from the too great love of things, but also from the too great love of friends and relations. That last stage could not have lasted long. It was simply a preparation for death, which could not tarry much before it released the wanderer (*parivrâjaka*) from his last enemy, and restored him to that bliss of which this life had so long deprived him.'

Though not fully suited to the present mode of existence in India the ideal provided by this scheme of life has great attractions for Hindus of more than average character and attainments. Men in all conditions of life strive to secure a period wherein to meditate and take thought for the life to come.

Mr. Javerilal Umiashanker Yajnik, of Bombay, Agent to H. H. the Rao of Cutch, in a work published in the early part of 1889, has written an interesting memoir of Gaorishankar Udayashankar, C.S.I., ex-Minister of Bháunagar, who is now in retirement as a *Samnyâssi*. The book is of value to all who are interested in India; it records the achievements of an Indian statesmen. Mr. Javerilal states that after his friend's retirement from the Dewanship of Bháunagar, 'he lived in his garden-house, situate outside the old town, at a distance from his house. This was something like residing as a Vânaprastha. While in this third Asrama he received friends and relations at his garden-house, and when referred to for opinion on matters of state, gave such advice as he thought proper. He tried, however, to divert himself more and more from worldly concerns. His name and the interest evinced by him in the Vedánt studies had drawn at times many an itinerant noted anchorite or *Samnyâssi* from Sringeri, Benares, Nepal, and other remote parts of India; and had extended the fame of Bháunagar as a home of Indian philosophical speculations in Káthiáwád and Gujarát. In July, 1887, finding himself advancing in years, and fearing lest he might leave this world whilst in the third Asrama, he resolved firmly to enter the fourth stage of a Brahman's life—that of a *Samnyâssi*.

During his active political career he had experienced the lights and shades of life in a high degree. He had enjoyed the sweets and bitterness of power, the smiles of fortune, the pleasures of hope, with some of the bitterness of disappointment. So far, while in the third stage, it was a life of holy living. His mind breathed sentiments of piety and of love of God. But he had a yearning after living in a world exclusively spiritual. Having reached the age of eighty-one, he thought the time had come when he should prepare himself for holy dying by a complete renunciation of the active concerns of this world and by exclusive devotion to the thoughts of the life to come. This was *Sanyás* or asceticism, or spiritual living of the highest order, as contemplated by the Hindu Shástras. As required by the Hindu religion, he first obtained the consent of the members of his family and his relations to carry out his purpose. He then wrote farewell letters to his friends, European and Native. The letter to the Thakor Saheb of Bháunagar, his master, he wrote in the most touching terms. It was the last letter that he wrote. It was full of gratitude for past favours and of sound advice for the future. For four days he underwent the ceremonies prescribed by the Hindu religion for reception into the holy order of a *Samnyássi*. He was named by his Guru "Sachchidánand Sarasvati". Hundreds and thousands of the people of Bháunagar and of the neighbouring villages proceeded to his Asram to offer their greetings to the venerable "Swámi". His Highness the Thakor Saheb of Bháunagar not only paid a visit to his aged ex-minister, but issued a proclamation announcing the event of Mr. Gaorishankar having entered upon the life of an ascetic, recounting his past actions, and paying a well-merited compliment to his exemplary public services and his still more exemplary life and character. The proclamation concluded by directing the closing of all public offices in Bháunagar for two successive days in memory of the event.[1]

Sir George Birdwood, in an Introduction which he has written to Mr. Sorabji Jehanghir's recently-published work on eminent Indian and Anglo-Indian personages and persons, tells a most entertaining story exhibiting a similar phase of character, which happened within his

---

[1] Dealing with regrets expressed by Sir William Wedderburn and others that the aged statesman of Bháunagar should have seen fit to wholly retire from public life, Mr. Javerilal says:—'These European friends of Mr. Gaorishankar were doubtless right from the standpoint from which they looked at the matter. They had common sense and worldly wisdom on their side. No country or community of men can well afford to dispense with its old men, who combine in themselves the experience and wisdom of years. Mr. Gaorishankar, however, looked at the question from a different standpoint altogether. He was not unwilling to give to the Ruler of Bháunagar, and to those around him engaged in the administration of the State, the benefit of his advice and judgment. But the question with him of all others was this: He had done a good life's work, having for full fifty-six years devoted his great intellect and good heart to the service of his master and the interests of the State, and had earned well-merited repose. Even in his retirement into private life, he had shown himself ever ready to forward the cause of good government. In his green old age he thought he had now left to him a few hours of the evening of life. Those few hours he wished to devote exclusively to the service of his Maker and to the contemplation of those problems of life and mind which were vividly brought to his notice by his study of the Vedántic philosophy. His mind had attained to a state of what is called "*Tívra vairágya*", or blessedness of dispassion, which made him think that in this world he owned nothing and he desired nothing. It must be borne in mind, again, that when he decided to become a *Samnyâssi*, his state of health appeared so precarious that he did not expect to live long. It was better, he thought, that he should cut himself adrift from this world and die a holy death as a *Samnyâssi* than as a worldly man. It was a mode of life best suited,

own experience. That portion which relates to the Hindu characteristic noted is as follows:—'And then the great hope of his life having been fulfilled, straightway a strange change came over' Jagonathjee Sunkersett. 'He was a man of strenuous energy, and the most masterful natural capacity, and undisguised ambition and pride. He was not only the leader of the Hindus of Bombay, but, after the death of the first Sir Jamsetjee Jejeebhoy, of the whole Native community. But now

according to him, to the attainment of the highest end he had in view. If, after this renunciation of worldly concerns, it pleased the Almighty to give him a longer lease of life, that would be no bar to the attainment of his object. In the exercise of power, in the enjoyment of riches, in the esteem of his fellow men, in the favour of his successive royal masters, in the good opinion of his Native and European friends, and in the high respect in which he was held by the British Government, he had perhaps attained to a measure of worldly happiness to which few men in his state and in his position could lay claim. But his soul soared higher and yearned after something more exalted, namely, that peace of mind which he looked for in vain in the stormy world of external phenomena. He sought for a different environment. In the inner consciousness of his soul he sought for a refuge from those irresistible external forces which carry a man with abrupt transition from the heights of joy to the depths of sorrow. These influences would work upon him as they would work upon any other person through *Avidyá*, or ignorance of what was the highest good. But having overcome this *Avidyá* by a knowledge of the highest good, the vital question of the hour with him was, how best to live in the blessedness of holy knowledge? To that vital question he had but one answer to give—an answer that alone could satisfy his mind. That answer was in the words of the "Mahábhárat":

> '"While yet thou art respited, care
> For things unseen, for death prepare;
> And sunk in meditation deep,
> The fruits of holy knowledge reap."[1]

'Thus his ethic of *Sanyás* or renunciation consisted in an attempt to reap the fruits of holy knowledge, and thereby attain to that state of blessedness on which his soul was bent.'

[1] Muir's Metrical Translations from the "Mahábhárat", p. 23.

he laid aside all worldliness, and unobtrusively and determinedly submitted himself to the great desire for death that seemed to have taken complete possession of him; saying, on my once venturing to remonstrate with him for thus yielding himself up to die, and in so saying using almost the very words of the Greek writer: "It is not difficult, Birdwood, but easy; for the road is not crooked but straight, and not up and then down, but all downward; and an unfearing man may walk it blindfold." No! he had seen the salvation of God, as sought by him; and now all he wanted was to depart in peace.'

Such influences as have been described above had their effect upon the mind of the Hindu Prime Minister of Nepal. Sir Ranadip Sing, as years passed and the natural limit of his life was nearing, devoted more of his time to pious devotions and less to public affairs. His grasp of administration relaxed. More and more he trusted his relatives, upon some of whom he had conferred important posts. Among those most favoured was Bir Shumshere, the eldest of several sons of Dhir Shumshere, the youngest brother of Sir Jung Bahadur, who, as has been seen, when Sir Ranadip Sing became Prime Minister, was made Commander-in-Chief. Dhir Shumshere died in 1884. Prior to his death he had sent his eldest son, Bir Shumshere aforementioned, to Calcutta. While in Calcutta Bir Shumshere attended, for a short while, some of the classes at Doveton College. Here he acquired a smattering of English and also a superficial acquaintance with European learning. His attainments are declared, by those who know him best, to be very poor. In no respect has he indicated the possession of a superior mind which would enable him to fittingly fill the position he has usurped. What he does possess, as his acts have shown, are the qualities which have ever been conspicuous in the Asiatic conspirator: cunning, duplicity, and relentless barbarity. Sir Ranadip Sing seems not to have read aright the character of his ambitious and crafty nephew. Honours were heaped upon that nephew, and positions of the highest importance were granted to him. He was Adjutant-General of the army, while his brother, Kharag Shumshere, was Minister for Foreign Affairs. It had been determined by the Prime Minister that Nepal should be represented at the Indian Government's Camp of Exercise at Delhi in the cold season of 1885-86, by a brigade of Nepalese troops. The command of this brigade was placed in the hands of Bir Shumshere, who was thereby enabled to tamper with their fidelity to the family of Jung Bahadur,—a fidelity which found remarkable expression in 1856. Dr. Oldfield, in his Sketches from Nepal,[1] tells the story. He says: 'Considerable excitement was created in the Durbar by the discovery that a jemadar of one of the Gurung regiments had been instigating many of his comrades to assassinate Jung Bahadur; and it was feared that a large number of the troops were involved in the conspiracy. A general parade of all the troops, artillery included, was ordered to be held on the Thandi Khel, at which it was at first intended that the Gurung regiments, if found to be mutinous, should be destroyed *en masse*. This plan was, however, given up, and the prisoner being brought on parade, proof of his guilt

[1] Vol. ii, pp. 19-20.

was produced, and the verdict of the different regiments was taken. On referring the case to the Gurung regiments, who were expected to sympathise with the prisoner, the men consulted together for some time, and then suddenly fell on him and cut him to pieces. They professed great attachment to Jung Bahadur, and indignation at the conduct of the man whose conspiracy, if successful, would have brought disgrace, for want of loyalty, on the whole of their tribe; they regarded him as a traitor, and treated him accordingly. The parade was then dismissed without any further disturbance.'

Bir Shumshere had so completely gained the affection and confidence of his uncle that permission was given to him to replace all inefficient officers in the brigade with others whom he deemed efficient. Further, the Prime Minister was induced to issue a proclamation in which it was declared that the troops were to implicitly obey the orders given to them by their new commander, and that disobedience would be followed by immediate death. The Minister was evidently anxious that the Nepalese troops should take their part in the manœuvres of the Indian army on the plains of Delhi worthily, and adopted this among other means of ensuring discipline. So many years had passed in Nepal without disturbance, that a sense of complete security filled Sir Ranadip Sing's mind. This circumstance made combination for the purposes of conspiracy and assassination easy.

During the evening of Sunday, November 22nd, 1885, while the aged Prime Minister was in his room engaged in his devotions, the nephew requited his uncle's confidence by basely murdering him. On this evening the soldiers of the brigade were ordered, on some pretext or other, to remain in camp, instead of, as usual, dispersing to their homes when the day's duties were done; they were furnished with ball-cartridges, which the conspirators were able, without any difficulty, to obtain from the military stores. Bir Shumshere and his fellow conspirators (including four of his brothers) provided themselves with fire-arms, and proceeded to the palace of the Minister, where they arrived between eight and nine. Bir Shumshere halted on the second floor, where the child-King and the Queen-Mother had their apartments, the rest of the conspirators proceeding to complete the deed. Sir Ranadip Sing was, as has been stated, engaged in devotional writing in a room on an upper floor. Near him was seated the Senior Dowager Queen, two other daughters of the late Jung Bahadur, an orderly officer of the Resident, and the Court newspaper reader. One of the conspirators knocked at the door, and, when asked his business, replied that he had to place an urgent despatch from the Viceroy of India before Sir Ranadip Sing. The door was opened, and Bir Shumshere's brothers entered. One of them went up forthwith to the Minister and fired. The ball only grazed his forehead. A second shot, fired by another brother, entered his skull, and Sir Ranadip Sing fell lifeless on the floor. The palace was immediately in an uproar.

Bir Shumshere, who had been waiting below to hear the report of the murderous shots, recognised that the conspiracy had succeeded. He immediately waited on the King and Queen-mother, ascribed the murder to General Ranabir Jung, who had nothing to do with the conspiracy, and, by working on their fears, persuaded them to accompany him to the camp. In the camp Bir Shumshere was master of the situation. An armed brigade was at his command. He proclaimed himself Prime Minister of Nepal by command of the King. Soldiers were despatched to Manohara and to Thapathali. At the first place Juggut Jung, and at the latter place Yudh Protap Jung, were murdered. The Prime Minister's son, Dhoje Nursing, and his nephews, Redar Nursing, Puddum Jung, and others, were pursued with implacable hatred, and it was only by taking shelter at the Residency their lives were saved. All the members of the Rana family in the hands of the rebels were closely imprisoned and tortured with ingenious cruelty, some seventeen faithful adherents of the family being also ruthlessly butchered. It is worthy of note, as indicative of the ruthlessness with which the revolution was conducted, that the murderers did not shrink from attempting the life of the Senior Dowager Queen, three shots having been fired at her; it was owing solely to the intrepidity of Dhoje Nursing, the Prime Minister's son, her nephew, that she was able to escape with her life.

General Dhoje Nursing himself describes the circumstances under which he was attacked and barely escaped with his life in these terms:—'Immediately after the murder of my lamented father, Sir Ranadip Sing, the conspirators took charge of the person of the minor King, and conveyed his Highness to the military encampment at Khatmandu. The troops having been called out, it was given out to them that the late Regent had been murdered by General Ranabir Jung and myself; that we had also designed the murder of his

Highness with the intention of subverting the existing dynasty; and that, to defeat our treasonable plans, his Highness had been removed to the camp for protection and safety. A proclamation in the King's name was read to the men, by which General Bir Shumshere was appointed Prime Minister, and the men were commanded to massacre the alleged murderers of Sir Ranadip as well as the other sons of Sir Jung Bahadur. The Nepalese troops, whose loyalty to the throne is almost a passion, were thus misled into assuming an attitude of determined hostility against us. The army having been secured, the whole country now lay at the feet of the revolutionists. The presence of the young Maharaj-Adhiraj in their midst also lent colour to their misrepresentation. Large numbers of soldiers were despatched to Manohara and Thapathali, where Juggut Jung, the eldest son of Sir Jung Bahadur, and his son Yudh Protap, were respectively residing, to massacre them; the misguided men executed the bloody mission only too faithfully. Another considerable force was also simultaneously despatched to accomplish my destruction and that of the remaining sons of Sir Jung Bahadur. I was at the time working in my office, but the commotion in the city, joined to the sudden appearance of some armed soldiers at my office gate, attracting my attention, I hurried homewards amidst a shower of bullets. I was not hurt, however; and when I got home, I was pressingly implored by my mother to save myself by flight. By this time my house was nearly surrounded by the soldiery, and being passionately urged by my mother, I escaped into the Residency. How I escaped is still a wonder to me. It could only be providential: and

GENERAL JUGGUT JUNG RANA BAHADUR,

ELDEST SON OF SIR JUNG BAHADUR—MURDERED BY BIR SHUMSHERE.

next to my God, I am thankful to the officers and men of the Residency for saving my life from the blood-hounds that were in pursuit after me.

'My life has been saved, but all my earthly possessions are gone. I entered the Residency with only my office dress on, and all the time I stayed there I had not another change of dress. And I left the Residency in the same destitute condition. Arrangements were made by which most of my exiled cousins received, if not the whole, at least a fair portion of their personal property. A different course, however, was pursued towards me, and I quitted home, friends, and country without receiving a single piece of silver out of my large paternal estate. Perhaps this harsh measure has been meted out to me as an opponent from whose popularity with the people of Nepal effective resistance was dreaded by the party in power. For it is a source alike of pride and gratification to me that, during my late father's premiership, I was instrumental both as his private secretary and as Commissioner of the Terai, in promoting many domestic reforms conducive to the welfare of my country.'

The *coup d'état* was successful. Several of the refugees, regarding the British Residency as a sanctuary, fled thither for safety. The Resident, Colonel Berkley, was absent, and the medical officer in charge of affairs. A subordinate officer, of no diplomatic experience, virtually decided the British Indian policy towards Nepal at this, perhaps the greatest, of her crises. Colonel Berkley, on his return, found a number of refugees within the precincts of the Residency. He treated them with great harshness. Instead of displaying kindness and exercising that power on their behalf which under the Treaty it is clear he ought to have displayed, he acted otherwise, and made Bir Shumshere's treachery and ferocity respectable by ensuring its success. There was a too pronounced tendency to uphold violence, due, evidently, to a fear of friction and possible hostilities arising from the assumption of a bolder and more honourable attitude. For days the Residency was surrounded by Nepalese troops—a menace to which a stronger man than Colonel Berkley would not have submitted for an hour longer than availed to remonstrate with the authorities and to demand their instant withdrawal. Generals Puddum Jung and Ranabir, and several of the refugees, were in a manner turned out of the place. Had they been allowed to stop a few days longer, there was every hope of the army being undeceived, and the revolution suppressed before it had made much headway. During a portion of the time the Royal refugees were at the Residency they had scarcely a morsel of food to eat, while the treatment of many of them throughout, by the acting Resident, was galling in the extreme. The King's uncle, Norendro Bikram Shah, sought protection at the Residency, and was, contrary to all British traditions, refused shelter, and was handed over to his enemies. While remaining at the Residency every possible attempt was made to induce the refugees to recognise the usurper and to accept the new condition of things. The Dowager Maharani, in a memorial which she presented for herself and others of the refugees to the Marquis of Dufferin, while that nobleman was Viceroy of India, said: 'After the massacre, Bir and Kharag Shumshere made your Excellency's memorialists considerable offers of money, and offered also to give up to your memorialists the whole of their property, subject to the ignominious condition of accepting the bloody revolution effected, and condoning the murders perpetrated, by the usurpers; but these seductive offers your Excellency's memorialists indignantly rejected, and they were in consequence not only prevented from bringing away their moveable property beyond a scanty portion of the same, but compelled in their utter helplessness —even for the purpose of saving the lives of their families and children, which were in imminent peril— to sign documents containing admissions and engagements which, in all loyalty to the Throne, to their country, and to truth, they are bound entirely to repudiate.' They added: 'Your Excellency's memorialists refrain from encumbering this memorial with details of the cruelties and indignities to which they and their families have been subjected, and of the unutterable enormities of which the subverters of the Government have been guilty. These they would prefer explaining to your Excellency in person, if favoured with an audience.'

The audience asked for was never given, as will appear in succeeding chapters. Lord Dufferin, apparently, knew nothing of the services so frequently eulogised by his predecessors, or of the claim which the royal and noble Nepalese had upon his best efforts. The Foreign Office, which knew all about it, and which should have been quick to enable the Viceroy to show that it was a wise and prudent thing on the part of Asiatic notabilities to display friendship towards the Indian Government, apparently refrained from telling

Lord Dufferin what he did not know. On no other hypothesis is the ex-Viceroy's conduct to be understood or explained.

CHAPTER VI.

A DOWAGER QUEEN: HER TREATMENT IN CALCUTTA.

It was a serious misfortune for the Nepalese friends of the British Government that Colonel Berkley was acting Resident in Nepal when the assassinations occurred. Had Mr. Girdlestone been at Khatmandu many incidents in this story—all the incidents which reflect on the Government of India—would not have happened. Mr. Girdlestone not only knew who were the real friends of the British Government in India, but he also knew what was demanded, in the way of firmness, on the part of the representative in Nepal of that Government. Colonel Berkley altogether misconceived the situation. It is true, whatever his knowledge of the circumstances of the country might be, neither he nor the Resident for whom he was acting could have prevented the acts of bloody usurpation. Bir Shumshere, and the faction at his back, were too strongly determined to test their power and realise their guilty ambitions to be thwarted in their attempts. Sir Ranadip Sing, it is certain, in any case, would have been assassinated, as also would other noblemen. If, however, the acting Resident had shown courage and readiness of resource, combined with a determination that Britain's friends should be supported by Britain's might and authority, and, further, had represented the facts to the Government of India in their true light, Bir Shumshere would have failed in his designs, the Rana family would have maintained its constitutionally rightful position in Nepal, the country itself would have been better governed than it has latterly been, and India's north-eastern frontier would have been rendered impregnable. All these things have been forgone. The diplomacy which allowed them to slip through its fingers is not to be congratulated on its prescience; rather is it to be condemned for its want of foresight and its conspicuous lack of high-minded qualities. On the other hand, Bir Shumshere has not consolidated his position. The country is in a condition of unrest. There has been either a rising or an attempt upon the Prime Minister's life nearly twice a year since he succeeded in his designs. He is coquetting with China.[1] The chances are that, ere many years be passed, the Government of India will find that they have to pay dearly

---

[1] 'A rumour, widely current in Nepal, has reached us to the effect that Bir Shumshere has concluded a secret treaty with China, which is said to be anything but favourable to the British alliance. The recent arrival of a Chinese Embassy at Khatmandu, almost simultaneously with the Sikkim-Thibetan *imbroglio*, seems to have a deeper political significance than one might ordinarily attach to it; and we would accordingly warn our Government to carefully watch the proceedings of the usurper, who, we are inclined to think, is unscrupulous enough, in the pursuit of his lawless ambition, to sacrifice the dearest interests of his country to personal aggrandisement. With Russia knocking at the North-West gate of India, the political activity of China on our northern frontier certainly wears a most suspicious appearance.'—*Indian Mirror*, October 15, 1888.——The same paper, writing thirteen months later, remarked that a rumour was widely afloat in Nepal that Bir Shumshere had executed a secret treaty with China, to the prejudice of the British alliance. It added: 'This may or may not be true, but, considering

for the want of judgment and courage shown by the acting Resident at Khatmandu when General Ranadip Sing was so foully murdered, and for the lack of courtesy and kindness displayed in Calcutta. General Dhoje Nursing and some of the other princes possess all the force and decision of character peculiar to high-born Khetriyas, born and bred in a perfectly free atmosphere; and they would, no doubt, have secured their own remedy ere this, but that their movements were at one time fettered by the Indian Government, which subjected them to a close police surveillance. They will not be idle, however, when the time for action comes. They are simply biding their time.

The British people, as a rule, are free enough with their sympathy for fallen monarchs, especially for royalties of the female sex. The ex-Empress Eugenie of France is still spoken of in England by the title she bore, and is treated with the most friendly regard by the monarch and aristocracy and the newspaper press of England. Far different from this or from anything approaching this was the treatment which the Senior Maharani of Nepal received from the Calcutta Foreign Office when her royal highness had occasion to com-

---

the man's antecedents, it is not at all improbable; and hence we felt it to be our duty to draw the attention of our Government to the matter. Our suspicions have been further strengthened by the prolonged stay of the Chinese Embassy at Khatmandu, who are said to have conveyed a broad hint to Bir Shumshere that Nepal is expected to discharge with fidelity its obligations to Thibet under the treaty of 1856, the second article of which provides: "That the States of Gurkha and of Thibet have both borne allegiance to the Emperor of China up to the present time. The country of Thibet is merely the shrine or place of worship of the Lama, for which reason the Gurkha Government will, in future, give all the assistance that may be in its power to the Government of Thibet, if the troops of any other Rajah invade that country." '

municate with that Department of the State. The usual form of address (a matter of the highest importance in an Oriental country) was denied to her, a denial which occasioned much annoyance not only to her royal highness herself, but to all her relations and friends.[1]

The Marchioness of Dufferin, in 1886, granted the Maharani an interview, and showed some little interest in her sad condition. For a time it appeared as if the

---

[1] The particulars of the marriage of the Dowager Queen when read in this connection seem the very irony of fate. To the younger members of the Calcutta Foreign Office the accompanying passages may be useful in teaching them the rank and position of the lady whom they treated and continued to treat with such slight courtesy until the autumn of 1889, when, Lord Lansdowne being Viceroy, a more courteous style was adopted towards her royal Highness. Dr. Oldfield gives a description of the marriage in these terms:

'1857, June 25th.—The King's eldest son, the heir-apparent, aged nine years, was married to Jung's eldest unmarried daughter, aged six years. The Resident and his suite were invited to be present officially, while the ladies were privately invited by Jung Bahadur to see the "tamasha" from his house. The Resident, etc., proceeded as usual to the Durbar, where they were invested by the King with an honorary "khilat". The King then led them out of the Durbar to the Hanuman Dhoka gate, where they were joined by the ex-King. The two kings then mounted one elephant, the Resident and his suite were on three more, while the rest of the King's retinue followed on elephants behind.

'About sunset the bridegroom was brought out in a gilt palanquin preceded by the "kalsa", carried amidst a crowd of slave-girls, and followed by his younger brother in another palanquin. Several regiments defiled out of the Kot and formed the van of the procession; after them came the band, then the "kalsa", followed by the bridegroom and his brother, and a long procession of elephants, the leading one carrying the two kings attended by the officiating minister, Khrishn Bahadur. The procession slowly wound its way past the Tallaju temple to the Indra Kot, whence turning to the right, it made a circuit and emerged from the city, at the north-west corner of the Thandikhel. Thence it slowly followed the high road, passed the magazine and Tripuri Punahari temple to Thappatalli, where it arrived between eight and nine o'clock. The road from the Durbar to Thappatalli was thronged throughout with spectators, and all the troops at the capital, about thirteen thousand in number, were present, either forming part of the

conduct of the vice-Queen of India towards the senior Maharani of Nepal would be marked by the cordial thoughtfulness shown by the Queen-Empress of India to the ex-Empress of France. The expectation was not realised.

Lady Dufferin's interest—owing, it is plain, to political pressure—soon ceased, and was transferred to the wife of Bir Shumshere, when that lady with her husband visited Calcutta two years later.

In her recently-published Selections from her

---

procession, or drawn up in masses, with about one hundred pieces of artillery on the parade. On reaching Thappatalli, the procession drew up in the courtyard, where it was joined by Jung Bahadur, who was very plainly dressed, and took no official part in the public proceedings of the day. After being again presented to the two kings, and receiving "rukhsat" (dismissal—leave to withdraw) from them, we were taken upstairs, still clothed in the shawls and turbans presented by the King, to the long room, where we joined the ladies and received some slight refreshment. We were then taken into the garden, where we saw some fireworks, and shortly after returned home. In the meantime the bridegroom and the rest of the marriage party went inside the private apartments, where the religious ceremonies of the wedding took place.

'On the following day, when the bridegroom had to bring back his bride to his father's house, the Resident and his suite had again to form part of the procession, while the ladies, as before, were invited by Jung to see the "tamasha" from his house. The procession was formed much in the same way as on the preceding day; first came the band, after it a long line of sweetmeats, ornaments, etc.; then the "kalsa" preceding the bride in a handsome gilt palki; after her came the bridegroom, then his brother, and after him a long line of elephants as before. The procession returned by the same route which it had followed the day before. Jung Bahadur escorted the ladies on an elephant, and accompanied the procession; but as he was not present officially, did not form a part of it. On reaching the Durbar we all dismounted, and were taken inside the quadrangle of the palace, where the ladies were introduced by Jung to the bride and bridegroom and to the two kings. We received our "rukhsat" from the King, and then returned home. On each of the two nights after we left there was a good deal of artillery and musket firing, and the festivities, dancing, etc., were kept up among the populace to a late hour. The bride was to remain one night at the Palace

Journal,[1] kept whilst in India, Lady Dufferin describes the interview which the Dowager Queen had with her. The Viceroy's wife writes as follows :—

'I do not know whether you have read about the revolution in Nepal and the murder of the Maharajah Sir Ranadip Singh, the Prime Minister and ruler, which took place last November. He was lying on a bed in a small room in his palace, when four of his nephews came in, and, pretending to show him a new rifle, shot him dead. His wife, the Bari Maharani, and the Jaitha Maharani, the mother of the real heir, took refuge in the Residency, went on into British territory, and are now in Calcutta. The Bari Maharani wrote and asked me to see them, and I was allowed to do so as an expression of sympathy with them in their grief. Unfortunately the widow was ill, and could not come, but the Jaitha Maharani, who saw the man shot, and who is also a widow, came, and a more extraordinary figure I never saw. Her appearance deserves minute description. My first view of her was that of a mass of light gauze above, and a pair of legs clothed in loose white trousers below. Having conducted this avalanche of gauze to a sofa, I

---

with her husband, and not five nights, as is usual with ordinary people; the next morning early she was accordingly taken back to Thappatalli. On the occasion of this wedding the King was very liberal in his presents: "khilats" and jewellery were given to every officer in the Nepalese army, and every servant in the employment of the Durbar received a present of some kind or other. The whole of these expenses are defrayed from the public treasury, and there was not, as on the occasion of the King's eldest daughter being married, any capitation tax raised on the people. The dowry of the bride, of course, is paid by her father.'

[1] 'Our Viceregal Life in India: Selections from my Journal, 1884-1888,' by the Marchioness of Dufferin and Ava, pp. 289-290, vol. 1. Murray, 1889.

had time to study details. The thin pink and yellow striped material was not a petticoat, and I am quite at a loss to imagine how it was put on, or how many hundred yards were in it. It looked just as if a great piece had been unrolled, and unrolled in a heap on the floor, and then picked up and half wound round and half carried by the wearer. When she sat down it was in a great fluff, and when she got up she took it in her arms, and it overflowed everything, except the trousers. The body was made tight, and she wore pink mittens on her hands. Another wonderful part of her was her head. Her hair is jet black, and it was combed up from the back, and two very great plaits were arranged across the front, one on the top of the other. She had a straight fringe, and one long thin corkscrew curl on each side of her face. On her cheek there was a large round red mark painted, and during the interview she kept putting her finger, wrapped in her handkerchief very carefully, first into the corner of one eye and then into the other. I really did not see that she was stopping her tears until later when she broke down a little more. Her brother, who wore uniform and a small round cap with a chin-strap, was very deaf. He and an English doctor who was interpreting for me stood in front. She and I sat side by side on the sofa, and the maid, who was dressed like her mistress and who had a terrible squint, stood behind. I spoke to the doctor, and the doctor whispered into the ear of the brother, who, folding his hands before him, whispered into the ear of his sister; and we none of us said much to the purpose.

'Then I took her hand and walked with her to the

top of the staircase, and then ran to a window to see how she would get her skirts into the carriage.'

It is a misfortune that this passage appears in Lady Dufferin's book. The description of the dress and manner of these royal visitors might have been fittingly given in a private letter: the details, seeing that they are made the subject of sarcastic observation, ought not to have been published. The want of sympathy exhibited by the Vicereine is only too faithful a copy of the conduct of the Viceroy, and—all the circumstances considered—is the last kind of conduct which one would have thought possible on the part of the invariably kindly and cultured Marquis and Marchioness of Dufferin and Ava. It is adding insult to injury to show such a spirit to the daughter of Sir Jung Bahadur: to the daughter of a man whose services were rated so high by successive Viceroys of India that they were never to be forgotten. It is clear that the Foreign Office was determined to stand by the assassin and the usurper, for Lady Dufferin was only 'allowed' to see the Maharanis 'as an expression of sympathy with them in their grief'. Transplant the incident and the characters from Europe to Asia, and the unkindness—to use the mildest word possible—of the Viceroy and Vicereine becomes manifest.

Her Royal Highness sent a Memorial to the Viceroy, couched in the following terms:—

May it please your Excellency,

It is now upwards of two years since the writer of this, the Senior Dowager Maharani of Nepal, and daughter of Sir Jung Bahadur, came to British India under most melancholy circumstances. The late Sir Ranadip Sing, Prime Minister of Nepal,

H.R.H. THE MAHARAJ-ADIRAJ OF NEPAL.

had been treacherously murdered by General Bir Shumshere and his brothers; and I myself, though a woman, had been shot at by them, and would have shared the same tragic fate but that I succeeded in escaping into the Residency by timely flight. With the aid of the Brigade stationed at Khatmandu, to whose command General Bir Shumshere had been appointed by the generous confidence of the late Prime Minister, the conspirators had killed General Juggut Jung and his son Yudh Protap; sent the leading Bhardars into captivity, or otherwise compelled them to seek protection at the Residency; and thus established a military despotism on the ruins of the constitutional Government of the country. In this unhappy situation, I determined to leave Khatmandu for British territory; and I am thankful that I was enabled to fulfil my intention through the friendly assistance of the Residency officers and men. But I had to leave behind me my only daughter, who is Heir-Presumptive to the throne of Nepal, as well as all my personal property, with the exception of the jewelleries I had on my person.

As the head of the Royal Family of Nepal during the minority of the Maharaj Adhiraj, I may be permitted to say a few words on the present situation. By the old laws of Nepal, the King only could appoint his ministers for carrying on the work of administration; but if the king happened to be a minor, as in the case of Rana Bahadur Shah, Grivan Yudh Bikram Shah, and Rajendro Bikram Shah, the authority to appoint ministers, as well as the control of the administration, was usually vested in a Regency, composed of the senior qualified members of the Royal family. This law was, during the Premiership of my father, Maharaja Sir Jung Bahadur, abrogated in favour of a settled rule of succession to the Ministry, which was solemnly accepted by the then reigning Sovereign, Surendra Vikram Shah, and his father, Rajendro Bikram Shah, and by all the Bhardars of the State. But neither under the old law, nor under Maharaja Sir Jung Bahadur's Rule of Succession, is General Bir Shumshere lawfully or constitutionally entitled to exercise the authority of the Durbar which he has assumed in his hands. The King is a minor, and could not have given him the power; of the three senior qualified members of the Royal family two, namely, the Senior Dowager Maharani and the King's uncle, are decidedly opposed to his elevation, and view his usurpation of power with the greatest distrust and consternation; while he stands only fifth on the constitutional roll of succession to the Premiership. Successful violence, therefore, is his only title to power; and if the British recognition is founded on that fact, then I submit, it is opposed to the Treaty of 1801, the 3rd Article of which provides as follows:—

'The principals and officers of both Governments will cordially consider the friends and enemies of either State to be the friends and enemies of the other; and this consideration must ever remain permanent, and in force, from generation to generation.'

Surely the men who murdered the Prime Minister of Nepal; who attempted the life of a member of the Royal family, viz., of the Senior Dowager Maharani (which is felony punishable with death under the law of my country); who have placed the King's uncle in captivity; and subverted the constitutional government of the State; can only be regarded as her greatest enemies. I would respectfully ask your Excellency to think for a moment, if these unhappy events had occurred in England, how would the British people, how would all lovers of constitutionalism, regard the perpetrators of the crime? It is true Nepal is not England, but that is all the more reason why the truest friends and allies of Nepal should openly discountenance all political violence subversive of established order and tranquillity in the State.

Since my arrival in British India my minor daughter, I deeply regret to say, has been married by the party in power, into an inferior family and to a person acknowledged to be devoid of education, against my wishes and in spite of my strongest objections as communicated to the Foreign Office. No exigencies of policy nor considerations of political advantage could be pleaded in justification of the measure; it was, apparently, deemed not enough to have separated mother and child, and so the cruel wrong must needs be crowned with a crueller one, in order to inflict deep pain and humiliation on the exiled mother, if not to overawe the people of Nepal by a show of the irresistible power of the wrongdoers.

It is now, as I have said, over two years since I came to British India, but I am sorry to observe that no provision whatever for my support has been made by the present Government of Nepal.

At the time of my departure from Khatmandu a promise in writing was extorted from me that I should not claim any personal property nor ask for maintenance during my residence in British territory; but, as the promise was given under compulsion, and without a consideration, it is, of course, not binding upon me. According to the established usage of my country, members of the Royal family, while residing in British India, have always been liberally supported at the expense of the State; and the Government of India has, in the past, benevolently interfered to secure for them fitting provision from the Durbar. What crime, what felony have I committed to merit a different treatment? Even the Junior Maharani of Rajendro Bikram Shah, although guilty of the grossest excesses, was amply provided for on her retirement to Benares. These considerations have induced me to seek the good offices of the great Government of India; and, therefore, in reliance on the friendship and amity which have long subsisted between it and our family I beg that your Excellency's Government will be graciously pleased to exercise its benevolent interference in securing a suitable maintenance for me and in recovering my personal property, which I left behind at Khatmandu, from the present Government of Nepal.

I remain, your Excellency's most obedient servant,

SRI PANCH,

Senior Dowager Maharani of Nepal.

168, Lower Circular Road, Calcutta, May, 1888.

Other correspondence followed. Letters were written to and received from the Foreign Office. One of the latter contained a proposal addressed to her Highness of a humiliating character. The letter runs thus :—

From the Junior Under Secretary to
the Government of India.

To the Jaitha Maharani of Nepal,
No. 168, Lower Circular Road, Calcutta.

Foreign Department } Dated Simla, the 28th September, 1888.

Madam,

In reply to your petition of the 7th September, 1888, I

am directed to inform you that your case has been represented to the Prime Minister of Nepal, and it has been ascertained that he is willing to do something for you. He has been requested to communicate with you direct in the matter, and I am to suggest that you should take an early opportunity of writing to him.

I have the honour to be, Madam,

Your most obedient servant,

(Signed) G. K. IRWIN,

Junior Under Secretary to the Government of India.

Bir Shumshere did communicate with her royal highness, but in a fashion that added insult to injury. The letter which he wrote was as follows:—

To her Royal Highness the Senior Dowager Maharani of Nepal.

After civilities, &c.,

Salutation from the Powerful-armed Maharajah Bir Shumshere Jung Rana Bahadur. I dissuaded your Royal Highness by all sorts of arguments from leaving Nepal, but in vain. Your Royal Highness had intended putting up with your brother Jat Jung, but this, too, you have not done. I learn with regret that your Royal Highness is now in difficulties. Therefore, should your Royal Highness be willing to accept half the allowance made to the ex-Junior Maharani, now at Benares, write to me to that effect. In other words, the ex-Junior Maharani gets Rs100 per mensem, and half of that, viz., Rs50, will be allowed to your Royal Highness. Should you be willing to accept this small sum, I will arrange for its remittance to your Royal Highness. Asir Badi 1945 Sambad 12, day 3. (Signed) B. B. S.

Conceive the British Foreign Office being made aware that such a document as the foregoing from the Government of France, in response to a friendly hint from itself, was being sent to the ex-Empress Eugenie! No British Minister would have allowed an exiled Empress to be insulted by an offer of less than one hundred francs a month for the maintenance of herself and of her household, without the strongest of protests.

In India, however, a Briton in office does not shrink from a course of action at which in his own country he would shrink aghast. This is more than a pity; it is a calamity. For a Government which permits itself to be flouted in such a manner becomes an object of scorn to the very parties to whom it displays such complacency. Her Highness the Dowager Maharani, with very little delay, sent a spirited reply to the Viceroy.

'I do myself the honour,' her Highness said, "to submit herewith a letter in original from General Bir Shumshere, together with a translation of the same for your kind perusal.

'It will be seen that General Shumshere has thought proper to offer me Rs. 50 per mensem by way of a suitable settlement for me—an offer which will speak for itself. I may be permitted, however, to remark that the ex-Junior Maharani to whom he alludes is the notorious she-wolf of Nepal, authoress of the terrible Kot massacre of 1846, whose crimes led to her expulsion from the city. But notwithstanding her enormities, the Durbar permitted her to leave Nepal with her jewellery and treasure, amounting to upwards of twenty lakhs of rupees; and the archives of the Benares Political Agency will show that she was also allowed to retain possession of about twelve lakhs in cash and jewels which her husband, Maharajah Rajendro Bikram Shah, had taken with him to the holy city. In addition to this ample provision for her maintenance, she has been in receipt of a special allowance of Rs. 1,200 per annum for *pan supari*.

'My case is an entirely different one. A voluntary exile, I left Nepal under circumstances which have been fully explained to your Excellency in my letter of the

1st June last. My grateful acknowledgments are due to your Excellency for interposing your good offices in my favour; and if they have elicited an insulting response from General Bir Shumshere, I regret it only as a convincing proof of his implacable hatred and vindictiveness towards me for refusing, in the exercise of my rights, to acquiesce in his unlawful usurpation of power. I am, however, strongly sustained by the hope that the Christian Government of India, in remembrance of the friendship which has long subsisted between it and my family, and also of the services rendered to it by my late father, Sir Jung Bahadur, will kindly continue its generous intervention in my favour until a suitable provision for my maintenance is secured from the present Government of Nepal. And in that fervent hope I now leave the matter in your Excellency's hands.'

It seems almost impossible to believe that so courtly and so generous-minded a man as Lord Dufferin is known to be could have allowed so insulting an offer to be made to her Highness. Possibly he did not know, and it may be no personal fault of his Excellency's that no reply has ever been sent to the memorial just quoted. It does not follow that if a memorial to the Viceroy of India is sent to him it necessarily reaches his Excellency's hands. The Indian Foreign Office and its Agents in various parts of India do not constitute a safe medium for the transmission of such documents. They exercise their own good pleasure as to whether the documents shall or shall not be delivered.[1]

One sad calamity which has befallen the Dowager

[1] Recent proceedings in connection with the feudatory States of Bhopal and Rewa furnish instances in proof.

Queen might have been avoided had the Foreign Office listened to the appeals addressed to it by her Highness. Soon after her arrival in Calcutta, the Maharani applied to Lord Dufferin to use his influence in procuring the restoration of her daughter, the Princess Royal of Nepal, to her custody and protection. The prayer was disregarded. On October 15, 1889, the leading Indian paper in Calcutta contained the following paragraph:—'We are sorry to learn that the Princess Royal of Nepal died lately in child-bed at Khatmandu. She had been safely delivered of a girl, but the after-pains, we are told, were exceedingly protracted and severe, lasting for about fourteen hours, and the young Princess succumbed to the pains,—a sad victim of the cruel neglect of those responsible for her care and safety. We beg to offer our sincere condolence to H.R.H. the Senior Dowager Maharani of Nepal on this melancholy occasion. The deceased Princess was her only daughter. Bir Shumshere detained the latter by force in Nepal, when the mother left her country for British territory after the outbreak of the late revolution.' The same paper remarks, with much appositeness:—'There now remains only another young life between Bir Shumshere and the the throne of Nepal. Will the inordinate ambition of the usurper be proof against the temptation of smothering that life, while it is in his power, and of securing the throne for himself, bereft, as it is now, of all its natural pillars by the exile and banishment of the leading Sirdars of the State?'

After the departure of Lord Dufferin, his successor, the Marquis of Lansdowne, was approached, not so much upon the main question as upon a subsidiary matter.

In other ways, however, than by communications from the Dowager Queen or General Dhoje Nursing, efforts were made to bring the facts before the present Viceroy's notice. There is hope that his Excellency may yet prove Lord Canning's executor and carry out the provisions of that distinguished nobleman's grateful assurances regarding Nepal and Sir Jung Bahadur.

In the autumn of 1889, a memorial, of which the following is a transcript, was sent to the Government of India:—

From

SRI PANCH,

SENIOR DOWAGER MAHARANI OF NEPAL,

To

His Excellency, the Most Honourable HENRY CHARLES KEITH PETTY FITZMAURICE, MARQUESS OF LANSDOWNE, G.M.S.I., G.C.M.G., G.M.I.E., etc., Viceroy and Governor-General of India.

53 Chowringhee Road, 10th October, 1889.

May it please Your Excellency,

It is with exceeding reluctance that I venture to trespass upon your Excellency's valuable time, but I am compelled to do so by circumstances of pressing necessity, which, I trust, will be my excuse for the present intrusion.

I understand that General Bir Shumshere purposes marrying the young Maharaj Adhiraj of Nepal to an illegitimate daughter of his; and that the marriage is to take place in a short time. If true, this would be a tyrannical exercise of power on his part without a parallel in the annals of any Hindu State, for the mother of the intended bride is a woman of a very low caste, whose children, under the Hindu law of marriage, are absolutely ineligible for marriage into the superior castes, much less into a Khetriya royal family. In these circumstances — rendered peculiarly unfortunate by the helplessness of the minor Maharaj Adhiraj, and of the junior Dowager Maharani, his mother, who, in their present isolation, dare not assert their voice in any matter —I venture, as the senior member of the reigning family of

Nepal, to beseech your Excellency to exercise your kind interference in preventing the proposed improper and degrading alliance.

I would further beg leave to invite your Excellency's attention to another matter of deep political significance. I understand that an Embassy from China has recently arrived at Khatmandu, apparently for the purpose of investing General Bir Shumshere with some Chinese title. But the arrival of the present Embassy, occurring as it does, almost concurrently with the Tibetan complication, suggests grave doubts as to the character of the mission with which it is charged; and, indeed, there are rumours abroad that General Bir Shumshere has concluded a secret treaty with China favourable to his own personal interests, but prejudicial to the British alliance. It has been the cherished policy of the statesmen of my country—beyond owning a nominal allegiance to China—to avoid cultivating any close political relations with that power, so that it might not, by any possible means, obtain the slightest foothold in Nepal; and hence the new departure is regarded with the gravest apprehension by the people, jealous as they always are of the presence of any foreigners in their midst.

With profoundest respect, I remain,

Your Excellency's most obedient and humble servant,

SRI PANCH,

Senior Dowager Maharani of Nepal.

With unusual promptitude, and, in a tone which indicated that Lord Lansdowne was taking a personal interest in the questions regarding Nepal which were addressed to his Government, the following reply was sent:—

From

THE SECRETARY TO THE GOVERNMENT OF INDIA

To

Her Highness, the JAITHA MAHARANI OF NEPAL.

Foreign Department } Dated Simla, the 23rd October, 1889.

Madam,

I am desired by his Excellency the Viceroy to acknowledge the receipt of your Highness's letter of the 10th inst.

Your Highness requests his Excellency's interference to prevent the proposed marriage of the Maharaj Adhiraj with a daughter of the Maharajah Bir Shumshere. The Government of India have, as Your Highness is aware, always abstained from interference with the domestic affairs of your family, and the Viceroy is unwilling, except for very strong reasons, to do anything inconsistent with the principles which have so long been accepted by the British Government. In the present instance His Excellency is informed that the mother of the Maharaj Adhiraj has given her consent to this marriage, and under the circumstances Lord Lansdowne does not consider that he would be justified in interfering for the purpose of putting a stop to it.

I am at the same time to express His Excellency's regret that he finds himself unable to accede to Your Highness's request, and I am to thank Your Highness for your information as to the arrival of a Chinese Mission in Khatmandu.

I have the honour to be, Madam,
Your most obedient servant,
(Sd.) G. K. Irwin,
For Secretary to the Government of India.

This communication, as will be seen, is couched in fairly courteous language and recognises the Maharani's title. Notwithstanding the refusal of the Viceroy to interfere in this instance, there is occasion—from Lord Lansdowne's admission that the Government of India may interfere in the affairs of Nepal if sufficient reasons exist—for taking a hopeful view of the future. Such a spirit in Viceregal circles four years earlier would have prevented nearly all the mischief described in these pages, and have saved the Government of India from many reproaches. It would seem from the letter quoted above that Lord Lansdowne, instead of being merely the mouthpiece of the Foreign Office, a mere registrar of the conclusions of 'permanent persons' who are the inheritors of the prejudices, and who are above all else loyal to the traditions, of The Office, is resolved to act for himself. It will be a good day for India and for the Indian Princes and people should this have happened.

The claims for assistance and goodwill on the part of the Government of India are of so clear a character and appeal so much much to all that is best in human nature and to all that is politic in administration, that the hopes which the Dowager Queen and General Dhoje Nursing repose in Lord Lansdowne can hardly fail to bear good fruit.

GENERAL DHOJE NURSING RANA BAHADUR.

CHAPTER VII.

A NEPALESE NOBLE'S FORTUNE.

The son of the man who fought for the British in 1857—General Dhoje Nursing—lost no time after his arrival in India in beseeching the good offices of the Government of India in securing for him his private fortune. Before troubling the Government itself, however, he wrote to the usurper in Nepal. In November, 1887, he addressed the Prime Minister of Nepal a memorial in which he recited the circumstances under which he left his country. He reminded Bir Shumshere that, immediately after the cruel murder of his late lamented father, Sir Ranadip Sing, he took refuge at the British Residency, unprovided with even a single change of linen, much less with any valuables whatever; and that, when he left Khatmandu, he did so without receiving a single farthing of his large paternal estate. His mother and stepmothers were, General Dhoje Nursing admits, allowed to bring away with them some jewellery of their own, and a sum of about two lakhs of rupees was also paid to them by way of compensation for private property with-held from them—the whole amounting, according to the high valuation of the new Administration, to seven lakhs of rupees. On his arrival in British India, Dhoje Nursing's mother most unselfishly placed her moderate fortune at his disposal, but this he found was quite inadequate to maintain him and his large family in ordinary comfort in a strange land where living is exceedingly dear. He added: 'My means have been much diminished by the heavy expenses I have been put to in providing medicines and medical comforts for my mother during her last protracted illness; in making, by her direction, numerous pious gifts for her spiritual benefit; and in performing her obsequial rites, and the *sradh* of my late father in the holy city of Benares. There are, moreover, now living with me a widow of Juggut Jung's and the son of Bhupendra Jung; and these are at present entirely dependent upon me for their support and maintenance. The elder Queen Dowager, the Jaitha Maharani, is also putting up with me, and I am bound in all loyalty and duty to the Throne to do my utmost to supply her Highness's wants in the absence of any provision whatever on the part of the Durbar to supply them. These burdens as well as my own I have to sustain with my daily decreasing resources. An exile from my native land, bereft of all the comforts, not to speak of the luxuries, I enjoyed at home, deprived of both my parents in the course of only six months—in one case under most tragic circumstances; when I contemplate these things, and, indeed, from what height to what depth I am fallen, a feeling of great dejection fills my mind, not so much on account of myself personally, as on account of the near and dear ones who depend upon me for their support and protection. In these circumstances I have been forced to address myself to your Excellency in hopes that the Durbar will be pleased to make over to me my paternal property, both moveable and immoveable, under such arrangements as your Excellency and the British Resident may approve. Herewith I beg to enclose a list of the said property, mainly framed from memoranda left behind her by my deceased mother; and I have only to request that, as she wrote the same from memory, the Durbar will be further pleased to grant me whatever excess might be found on verification of this inventory.'

The inventory is worth quoting in full, not only for more complete understanding of the matter on the part of the reader, but also as a matter of interest to English people, showing, as it does, the extent and character of the wealth of a leading nobleman in an Asian Kingdom.

The particulars referred to are thus set forth:—

INVENTORY OF THE LATE MAHARAJAH SIR RANADIP SING RANA BAHADUR'S ESTATE, MOVABLE AND IMMOVABLE, AT THE TIME OF HIS MURDER.

No. of items.	Particulars.	Amount in Indian Rs.
	MOVABLE ESTATE.	
1	Old gold coin 13,000 pieces @ Rs. 30 each..	3,90,000
2	Nepal ,, ,, 3,000 ,, @ Rs. 22 each..	66,000
3	Indian Rupees	23,00,000
4	Nepal ,, ...	5,00,000
5	Gold and Silver bullion	3,50,000
6	Head-dress or Pugri with large brilliants, rubies, etc...	2,50,000
7	Emerald Kantha or necklet consisting of 14 large Emeralds	72,000
8	Sword with handle set with diamonds ..	8,000
9	Belt, Scarf, etc. ,, ,, ...	21,000
10	One pair diamond bangles	22,000
	Carried forward—	39,79,000

No. of items.	Particulars.	Amount in Indian Rs.
	Brought forward—	39,79,000
11	One pair diamond bangles, armlets ..	25,000
12	Pearl necklet with diamond pendants ..	21,000
13	Ruby ring	9,000
14	One diamond and one sapphire ring ..	7,500
15	Emeralds supplied by my late mother for the Maharaj Adhiraj's head-dress, but not paid for..	51,000
16	Gold and silver plate, etc., for the late Maharajah and his family	70,000
17	Silver plates, etc., for about 170 guests ..	2,00,000
18	ASHBAB, including watches, watch chains, gold hubble-bubbles, Pan and atardans, gold and silver articles used in worship and for domestic purposes, curios, Guj motis or pearls, ivory collection, palace furniture and wardrobe, etc., etc. ..	9,00,000
19	Gold for making ornaments in goldsmith's hands	17,000
20	Swords, guns and rifles of various sorts, kookeries, elephants' howdars and appliances for *shikar*	2,00,000
21	Carriages, palkis, tamdans, doolies, etc. ..	35,000
22	*Sthreedhan* or cash belonging to my mother and stepmothers :— To my late mother Rs. 5,00,000 Three step-mothers ,, 4,00,000 Total .. Rs. 9,00,000 Deduct amount paid when leaving Khatmandu.. .. .. Rs. 2,00,000	7,00,000
23	Jewellery belonging to my step-mothers, wife, and children, not made over to them: TO MY FIRST STEP-MOTHER: Diamond flowers, Pearl necklace } Rs. 39,000 TO MY SECOND STEP-MOTHER. Diamond flowers and Pearl necklace Rs. 45,000 Emerald and Pearl Earrings } ,, 4,000 Rs. 49,000	
	Carried forward—	62,14,500

No. of items.	Particulars.	Amount in Indian Rs.
	Brought forward—	62,14,500
	To My Third Step-Mother.	
	Diamond flowers Rs. 7,500	
	Pearl Necklace ,, 4,500	
	Earrings ,, 2,500	
	Bangles ,, 1,500	
	Diamond and Emerald Rings ,, 3,200	
	Rs. 19,200	1,07,200
	Jewellery belonging to my Wife, Daughter, and Daughter-in-Law.	
	5 Diamond flowers Rs. 25,000	
	5 ,, necklaces ,, 36,500	
	20 Ruby choories ,, 2,000	
	20 Emerald ,, ,, 1,000	
	5 pairs Pearl earrings ,, 20,000	
	85,000	85,000
24	*Kaski Pokhola*, or the late Maharajah's allowance for one year, undrawn at the time of his murder. Rs. 1,10,000	
	Pay of Dhoje Nursing due for one year 30,000	
	Total Rs. 1,40,000	1,40,000
	IDOLS.	
	(Most rare and, therefore, hard to value.)	
	Lakshmi Narayanji	
	Ban Lingum	
	LIVE CATTLE.	
	100 Elephants	
	7 Musts:	
	Narayan Guj .. Rs. 25,000	
	Bullam ,, .. ,, 19,000	
	Ratan Prasad .. ,, 18,000	
	Soonder Guj .. ,, 16,000	
	Bursay .. .. ,, 13,000	
	Moti Prasad .. ,, 12,000	
	Carried forward—	65,46,700

No. of items.	Particulars.		Amount in Indian Rs.
		Brought forward—	65,46,700
	Hira Guj ..	.. ,, 10,000	1,13,000
15	MOOLAGAS:		
	Tilak Prasad Doorga ,, Raj ,, Ran Gumbhir Guj Maharaj ,, Sreo Persad ,, Sanoo Hira ,, Hanuman ,, Doar ,, Soonder (tuskless) Hira Prasad Lutchmi Prasad Mohun Guj Padam Prasad Sanu Bijily	15 @ Rs. 7,000 each	1,05,000
11	MUZHOLAS:		
	Lal Guj Bhairub Prasad Run Guj Meghnad Vena Prasad Hurruck ,, Nursing ,, Prem Guj Dhir ,, Pyar ,, Damar ,,	11 @ Rs. 3,500 each	38,500
42	FEMALES:		
	Champ Kali Nursing ,, Jahar ,, Damar ,, Pavan Begi	5 @ Rs. 4,000 each	20,000
	Chutter Kali Nayan ,, Hira ,, Manrupi ,, Baj Begi Lal ,, Tri ,,	7 @ Rs. 3,000 each	21,000
		Carried forward—	68,44,200

No. of items.	Particulars.	Amount in Indian Rs.
	Brought forward—	68,44,200
	Mangal Kali, Rupan ,, Vishnu ,, Sona ,, Gambhir ,, Bitchi ,, Gooman ,, Soogha ,, Kedar ,, Jan ,, Shib ,, Padam ,, Maharaj ,, Syam Begi, Laksh ,, Hyder ,, Soonder ,, Dhir ,, Pan ,, Doar ,, Ran ,, Kamal ,, Jung ,, Harihur ,, Golap ,, Pavan Poori, Jugut Rupi, Sooknayani, Mooniah, Motimala — 30 @ Rs. 2,000 each	60,000
	25 common ones @ Rs. 1,500 each ..	37,500
	43 HORSES	
	For riding.	
	Arabs: "Sheth" Bay Rs. 10,000	
	"Pahalwan" Chestnut ,, 2,600	
	"Wrangler" Irongrey ,, 2,500	
	"Amir" Chestnut ,, 2,300	
	One ,, ,, 2,200	
	,, Black ,, 2,000	
	,, Grey ,, 1,900	
	,, Copper Grey ,, 1,900	25,400
	Carried forward—	69,67,100

No. of items.	Particulars.		Amount in Indian Rs.
	Brought forward—		69,67,100
	Walers — One Chestnut ,,	2,200	
	Walers — ,, Bay ,,	2,200	
			4,400
	Tartar — "Moti" Grey ,,	700	
	Tartar — "Lakhay" Iron Grey ,,	600	
	Tartar — One Dun ,,	600	
	Tartar — ,, Black ,,	500	
	Tartar — ,, Bay ,,	500	
			2,900
	Pumi — One Bay ,,	600	
	Pumi — ,, Roan ,,	400	
			1,000
	Chanta — Two Piebald ,,	1,600	
	Chanta — One Grey ,,	600	
	Chanta — One Dun ,,	500	
			2,700
	For Carriages.		
	9 pairs Walers ,,	30,000	
	2 pairs Country ,,	800	
			30,800
	COWS:		
	60 Australian, Guzerati and Hurriani .. .. ,,	6,000	
	100 Chowry and Burmese @ Rs. 75 each .. .. ,,	7,500	
			13,500
	BUFFALOES:		
	35 Lahori		1,400
	SHEEP:		
	About 8,000 Doombas, Bhootias, and Burwals, etc.		24,000
	DOGS:		
	10 English Fox-hounds Rs.	3,000	
	9 ,, Grey ,, ,,	2,000	
			5,000
	IMMOVABLE ESTATE.		
1	The late Maharajah's palace at Narayanhitty with the grounds attached		16,00,000
2	Kalu Kazi's house and lands at Tookchapali		16,000
	Carried forward—		86,68,800

No. of items.	Particulars.	Amount in Indian Rs.
	Brought forward—	86,68,800
3	Garden at Burrawah 56 biggahs .. .. (Value not known)	
4	Garden at Pahgoo in charge of Captain Narbir Khettrya (Value not known)	
5	Garden (Tea) near Beejapore in Eastern Terai and hill in charge of Col. Hurro Lal Pandey. Annual yield Rs. 40,000	
6	Garden (Tea) at Nawalpore in charge of Captain Bukhan Sing. Annual yield ,, 40,000	
7	Estate at Pursa, Sirlie Mohattary and subtary in charge of Bamdev Pundit. Annual profits from plantation ,, 55,000	
8	Estate at Udeypore in charge of Captain Kanak Bahadur. Annual profits from plantation ,, 94,000	
9	Estate at Cheetown in charge of Col. Devi Bahadur. Annual profits from plantation ,, 25,000	
10	Estate in Koorary Pergunnah, Mohattary, in charge of Captain Jeetman Khettrya. Annual profits from plantation ,, 16,000	
11	Estate at Morung in charge of Captain Dasarut Padhya. Annual profits from plantation ,, 11,000	
12	Estate at Morung in charge of Soobah Deval. Annual profits from plantation ,, 4,000	
13	Plantation on the banks of the river Nuckoo in charge of Dittha Chatthay Newar. Annual profits ,, 1,400	
14	Plantation at Bhadgaon in charge of Col. Devi Bahadur. Annual profits from No. 1 Nepali Rs. 4,800 No. 2 ,, ,, 2,100 Total N. Rs. 6,900, Indian Rs. 5,520	
	Carried forward—	86,68,800

No. of items.	Particulars.		Amount in Indian Rs.
	Brought forward—		86,68,800
15	Plantation at Bhadgaon in charge of Dittha Chattay ,,	720	
16	Estate at Chandpooker in charge of Captain Jadunath Padhya. Annual Profits ,,	1,000	
17	Estate at Lal Pursa ,,	1,500	
18	,, Dookoo ,,	1,500	
19	Jaygir at Golaghat ,, (Granted to the late Maharajah for his services during the Indian Mutiny of 1857.)	7,000	
20	Sundry small parcels of land bought of Kuver Sahoo, Sakhoo and others. Annual profits ,,	500	
	TOTAL ANNUAL PROFITS—Rs. 3,04,140		
	Estimating the value of the above estates at sixteen years' purchase, the annual profits Rs. 3,04,140, give..		48,66,240
	Grand Total Rupees ..		1,35,35,040

(Sd.) DHOJE NURSING RANA BAHADUR.

29 November, 1887.

The refugees had no more earnest and disinterested friend than the late Mr. Girdlestone, Resident at Khatmandu. He, early in 1888, was in Calcutta, and favoured General Dhoje Nursing and the Senior Maharani with his counsel. In consequence of advice given by Mr. Girdlestone a letter was addressed to the Secretary to the Government of India, Foreign Department, by General Dhoje Nursing, in which he enclosed a copy of his letter to the present Prime Minister of Nepal, asking for the restitution of the estate of his late father, Maharajah Sir Ranadip Sing, as per inventory thereto appended. No reply to his letter being received, he handed, in December, a copy of the same to Mr. Girdlestone, with an earnest request that he would be good enough to lay it before his Excellency the Viceroy and Governor-General in Council, and move his Excellency to exercise his generous interposition with the Nepal administration on his behalf. The General proceeds:—'Presuming that these papers were duly laid before His Excellency, may I request the favour of your kindly informing me if any, and what, decision has been arrived at by the Government of India in reference to my claim against the Nepal Durbar? My father, equally with my uncle, Maharajah Sir Jung Bahadur, was unswervingly loyal and faithful to the British Government; and I, therefore, earnestly trust and hope that, in recognition of the fidelity of my family, His Excellency the Viceroy in Council will be graciously pleased to promote the recovery of my paternal estate. The benevolent interference of the British Government in promoting such settlements is not without precedent in the past; and I venture to think that it can scarcely be pretended by the ruling party in Nepal that, under the law of the land, my right and title to my paternal property has been in the least affected by the recent change of administration in the State. These considerations have inspired me with confident hopes of assistance from His Excellency's Government, strong as it is with the moral strength of an eminently able, just, conscientious, and high-souled *personnel*; and, relying on such generous support, I leave the matter in his Excellency's hands.'

At the same time a Memorandum dealing with the

whole question of the banishment of the Senior Maharani and of the family of Sir Ranadip Sing, and making suggestions as to the manner in which the Government of India could usefully interfere in Nepalese affairs, was drawn up by the General. It is an able document, and is in the following terms:—

'MEMORANDUM.

'I presume that the Government of India is now in possession of accurate information regarding the facts and circumstances connected with the recent Revolution in Nepal. Assuming this to be the case, it would be sufficient to mention that, immediately after the murder of my lamented father, Sir Ranadip Sing, the conspirators took charge of the person of the minor King, and conveyed his Highness to the military encampment at Khatmandu. The troops having been called out, it was given out to them that the late Regent had been murdered by General Ranabir Jung and myself; that we had also designed the murder of his Highness with the intention of subverting the existing dynasty; and that, to defeat our treasonable plans, his Highness had been removed to the camp for protection and safety. A proclamation in the King's name was read to the men, by which General Bir Shumshere was appointed Prime Minister; and the men were commanded to massacre the murderers of Sir Ranadip as well as the other sons of Sir Jung Bahadur. The Nepalese troops, whose loyalty to the throne is almost a passion, were thus misled into assuming an attitude of determined hostility against us. The army having been secured, the whole country now lay at the feet of the revolutionists. The presence of

GENERAL YUDH PROTAP JUNG RANA BAHADUR,
SON OF JUGGUT JUNG, AND GRANDSON OF SIR JUNG BAHADUR—MURDERED BY BIR SHUMSHERE.

the young Maharaj Adhiraj in their midst also lent colour to the misrepresentation. Large numbers of soldiers were despatched to Manoara and Thapathali, where Juggut Jung, the eldest son of Sir Jung Bahadur, and his son Yudh Protap, were respectively residing, to massacre them; and the misguided men executed the bloody mission only too faithfully. Another considerable force was also simultaneously despatched to accomplish my destruction and that of the remaining sons of Sir Jung Bahadur. I was at the time working in my office, but the commotion in the city, joined to the sudden appearance of some armed soldiers at my office gate attracting my attention, I hurried homewards amidst a shower of bullets. I was not hurt, however, and when I got home I was pressingly implored by my mother to save myself by flight. By this time my house was nearly surrounded by the soldiery, and being passionately urged by my mother, I escaped into the Residency. How I escaped is still a wonder to me! It could only be Providential; and, next to my God, I am thankful to the officers and men of the Residency for saving my life from the blood-hounds that were in pursuit after me.

'My life has been saved, but all my earthly possessions are gone. I entered the Residency with only my office dress on, and all the time I stayed there I had not another change of dress. And I left the Residency in the same destitute condition. Arrangements were made by which most of my exiled cousins received, if not the whole, at least a fair portion, of their personal property. A different course, however, was pursued towards me, and I quitted home, friends, and country without receiving a single piece of silver out of my large paternal estate. Perhaps this harsh measure has been meted out to me as an opponent from whose popularity with the people of Nepal effective resistance was dreaded by the party in power. For it is a source alike of pride and gratification to me that, during my late father's premiership, I was instrumental, both as his private secretary and as commissioner of the whole of the Terai, in promoting many domestic reforms conducive to the welfare of my country.

'In November last, I wrote to General Bir Shumshere, asking for the restitution of my property, but I have not yet received a reply. A copy of my letter was also given to the Resident, and I would solicit a reference thereto for particulars of my claim.

'For his services during the Indian Mutiny, the British Government was pleased to honour my father by making him a Knight of the Most Exalted Order of the Star of India. His subsequent career as Regent was also similarly marked by warm friendship and loyalty to that Government, numerous proofs of which no doubt exist in the archives of the Foreign Office. By those services and that proved loyalty, then, I appeal to his Excellency the Viceroy in Council for his generous interposition in securing to me the restoration of my paternal estate.

'I have so far dwelt upon a matter personal to myself, but the interests of my country demand from me a few words regarding the present situation. In submitting these humble views for his Excellency's gracious consideration, I do not in any way pretend to claim any special merit for them other than as being the outcome of an intimate knowledge of my countrymen, acquired both by personal contact with them and in the course of my long official connection with the Prime Minister's office.

'The Government of Nepal, before Sir Jung Bahadur's accession to power, was an absolute monarchy, the power of the King being only limited by certain injunctions in the Hindu shastras, which at best are vague and far from being of an obligatory character. All the evils incidental to despotism thus found a thriving soil in the country, the prosperity and advancement of which was proportionately retarded. It was Maharajah Sir Jung Bahadur who, with the assent of all the Estates of the realm, introduced a Constitution, which, while it upheld the dignity and supremacy of the Crown, at the same time curtailed the power of the Sovereign by vesting all executive authority in the hands of his ministers. This Constitution also regulated the order of succession to the premiership. General Bir Shumshere's assumption of the office of Prime Minister being a direct infringement of it, the question arises whether, in exercising the functions of that office, he has any other title to obedience than that of military predominance, built upon a misconception and mistake of the army. The King is a mere boy of thirteen, incapable of thinking and acting for himself, while there is reason to believe that most of the members of the Royal family are opposed to the present administration. The popular lull may be simply deceptive; at any rate it is no conclusive proof of acquiescence in the present situation. There is, moreover, disunion amongst the authors of the revolution themselves, and it may burst into a blaze any day. The turbulent classes of the population are also showing signs of activity, the example of successful violence, doubtless, acting as a stimulus to them. Here, then, are seeds of disorder, which may spring into a harvest of evils, destructive of order and good government in the State. Nepal's only hope of exemption from these threatened evils, therefore, lies in the beneficent interference of the British Government. The suzerainty of China over her is but a paper relation, and there is nothing, to my thinking, to restrain its friendly interposition. If this view of the situation be correct, then the best solution of the difficulty would seem to lie in the Government of India constituting a regency composed of the senior members of the Royal Family, namely—the elder Queen Dowager, the Queen mother, and the King's uncle. Female regencies are not unknown in the annals of Indian History, and no objection on that score can apply in the present case, as during the minority of Run Bahadur Shah, Nepal was governed by a regency consisting of the Queen-mother and Bahadur Shah, the King's uncle. A regency constituted in the manner suggested would, I am persuaded, be thoroughly acceptable to the army, the nobility, and the people. By this arrangement, the rights and privileges of royalty would be secured, while there would be little room for those political jealousies and consequent intrigues for the possession of power amongst the Bhardars, which have so often led in the past to immense bloodshed in Nepal. The power of appointing high ministers of State, and the control of the army, should be vested in this regency, to strengthen whose hands, however, the presence of a sufficient British force would be necessary at Khatmandu. As the Nepalese are exceedingly jealous of foreign interference in their domestic affairs, there should be an express understanding—to be embodied in a separate treaty—for the withdrawal of the British contingent on the King's attaining his maturity and assuming the reins of Government in his own hands. This, it seems to me, would be a satisfactory solution of the present difficulty. The presence of the British force would be a guarantee of protection to the loyal and the obedient; it would effectually repress individual ambition; give confidence to the timid and firmness to the wavering; and extinguish party animosities, unhappily so prevalent in the country, to the ruin of its best interests. General Bir Shumshere may not, perhaps, approve this scheme, as involving his temporary dislodgment from power; but if he be the able statesman and patriotic minister he is represented to be, he would no doubt come to the fore by sheer dint of ability and force of character. But whether he approve this scheme or not, personal interests should not, I submit, stand in the way of the public weal.

'In conclusion, I am authorized by her Highness the elder Queen Dowager to state that the scheme now submitted has her entire approval. I have here given a mere outline of my scheme; if the principle be approved, the details might be filled up in consultation with experienced officers of the State.

(Sd.) 'DHOJE NURSING RANA BAHADUR.

'*4th February*, 1888.'

All appeals, however, were in vain. The Government of India turned a deaf ear to every memorial of the kind. This is, perhaps, the more surprising, as one member at least of the Viceroy's Council regarded the action taken by Dhoje Nursing with favour; but, for various reasons, he was not able to secure for these friends of England due consideration.

In the meanwhile the Prime Minister of Nepal visited Calcutta, and was received with honour by Lord Dufferin. It is probable the claims of the refugees were mentioned during the conversations which the Foreign Secretary had with the Nepalese visitor. If so, the claims were not urged with much force, and Bir Shumshere's disclaimer of any responsibility towards the families of the men he had murdered was accepted.

In February of last year General Dhoje Nursing again addressed Sir Henry Mortimer Durand, the Foreign Secretary to the Government of India. He had received a brief letter from the Junior Under Secretary stating that when General Dhoje Nursing's claim was mentioned to Bir Shumshere that gentleman declined to assist, and did not admit any money to be due.

'I do not,' said the General in reply to this remark, 'want any help from General Bir Shumshere; I simply claim a restitution of my property, which all Nepal knows he seized by violence and retains possession of by force. That General Bir Shumshere would deny my claim is a matter of course; but it is notorious that he has not paid me a single farthing of my property yet.

'When I was staying at the Residency after the revolution, the then acting Resident, Colonel Berkley, advised me to come to British India, telling me that my property would be made over to me on my arrival here. A reference to the Residency records at Khatmandu will,

I doubt not, show that General Bir Shumshere did make an offer to that effect, and the Residency officers will prove that I received nothing from him when leaving Nepal.

'My father fought for the British Government as second in command of the Nepalese force during the Indian Mutiny: he was also unswervingly faithful to the British alliance during the period he was Prime Minister and Regent of Nepal. This, I respectfully submit, gives me a moral title to claim the sympathy and assistance of the Government of India. My Sovereign being a minor, and all power being in the hands of a usurper, I am not unreasonable in appealing to my Sovereign's powerful ally for help in my present difficulty under clause III. of the Treaty of 1801.

'General Bir Shumshere is virtually a creation of the British Government, but for whose recognition and support he would have been swept away long since. This being so, I humbly submit that the Government of India, in supporting him, has made itself responsible to the people of Nepal for the good government of the country during the minority of its ally; and hence it cannot justly withhold its interference when any glaring instances of gross injustice and wrong-doing are brought to its notice. General Bir Shumshere knows this but too well, and will never venture, I am sure, to refuse any just recommendation of the Government of India. Under this strong belief I appeal to His Excellency the Viceroy and Governor-General of India in Council to graciously exercise his influence in securing the rendition of my paternal estate from General Bir Shumshere.'

The General had an interview with Sir Mortimer

Durand. The following is the purport of the conversation that took place between them:

(After compliments)

Sir M. Durand: I think you have an ample fortune, General.

The General: Yes, if my expectations count for anything. But, you know, Sir Mortimer, that I have not received a farthing of my patrimony, and what I have got is only my mother's *streedhan*, which she was allowed to bring with her to India.

Sir M. Durand: And that must be considerable, isn't it?

The General: Yes, to an absolutely poor man. But, remember, that I have got *one* instead of *one hundred*, and to that extent I am, of course, the poorer. But the question is, not whether I have any means of my own at present, but whether I am not entitled to the support of the British Government in recovering my paternal estate from General Bir Shumshere.

Sir M. Durand: You must admit that we saved your life; but, unfortunately, we can't interfere further.

The General: I am deeply grateful to your Government for preserving my life; but, at the same time, I cannot understand what prevents you from interfering to get me my property, when you could interfere to save my life.

Sir M. Durand: No, we can't interfere in that direction, just as we can't interfere with either Scindhia or Holkar when he kills any of his subjects and seizes their property.

The General: But you forget, Sir Mortimer, that

General Bir Shumshere is not the Sovereign of Nepal, and only holds power by sheer brute force. My Sovereign is a minor, and hence my appeal to his ally, the British Government. If my own Sovereign had confiscated my property, I would not have sought your interference.

Sir M. DURAND: Well, a time may come when it will be possible for you to get your own. That eventuality, however, is not in the near future.

The GENERAL: I thank you for the hope thus held out to me. For my part I will not cease to trouble you till that hope is realized.

The General submitted his case to the Foreign Office for reconsideration in the letter which has already been quoted. The General also wrote to Sir Donald Mackenzie Wallace, requesting an interview with the Viceroy, but his request was refused on the plea of Lord Dufferin's time being too fully occupied to admit of compliance therewith.

Here, for the present, the matter ends. The Government of India has done nothing, and, except for an exhibition of courtesy on the part of the Marquis of Lansdowne, apparently intends to do nothing. In the face of the neglect to help friends of perilous times who are now in sore distress, and who are smarting under the deprivation of their private property, who can wonder that the Royal lady and these Nepalese nobles should turn to the correspondence of the Governor-General of India in 1858, and, as they read, wonder whether the English language is to be read contrariwise, whether in ordinary State affairs words are to be understood in a non-natural sense? They see Lord Canning's emphatic words of gratitude to Jung Bahadur. They note that he said 'the friendly consideration of his Government and the exertions and successes of his troops would be held in grateful recollection not less in England than in India.' India, they find, with a changed generation of officials, has lost memory of those striking services. Lord Canning's gratitude is, apparently, a matter for himself alone. His successors do not seem to consider it their duty to link themselves to it and carry out the behests to which the great ruler's word was pledged. Yet what Lord Canning placed on record was the judgment of the Government of India and not the judgment of the nobleman who, for the time being, happened to be Viceroy. These friends of ours find Lord Dufferin acting in a wholly contrary sense to Lord Canning, acting as though no promise were on record, as though no service had been performed. Lord Lansdowne, so far, has not repaired the harm done by his predecessor.

Who shall be surprised that, as they remember the words of the Prince of Wales, spoken in Nepal in 1875, that England never forgot the services Jung Bahadur rendered during the Mutiny, they ask whether the Royal word is a thing to be trifled with', and the spoken thoughts of a great Prince to be considered of no account?

From the Government of India they appeal to the British public and the British Parliament, with the confident hope that official memories are fresher in England than they appear to be in India, and in the steadfast reliance that England has not forgotten claims of gratitude publicly acknowledged and frequently ratified.

Will the Senior Dowager Queen of Nepal, the son of Sir Ranadip Sing, and the relatives of Sir Jung Bahadur make their appeal in vain?

APPENDIX.

I.

NEPAL AND CHINA: A POSSIBLE PERIL.

(*Indian Daily News, Oct.* 16, 1889.)

The *Indian Mirror* writes of 'a rumor widely current in Nepal, that Bir Shumshere has concluded a secret treaty with China, which is said to be anything but favourable to the British alliance,' and refers to the recent visit of a party of Chinese officers to Khatmandu as though it were a suspicious incident pointing to mischievous intrigue against British interests. There is nothing new, however, in the claim that China is suzerain of Nepal. It is a very convenient kind of overlordship, that does not concern itself with the internal affairs of the vassal's State, but leaves its independence practically complete while constituting an obstacle, to which Nepalese statesmen cling with strong affection, against the chance of annexation to India. Nepal pays tribute to China, and is careful to maintain the relationship, not because it is of any direct benefit, but because Chinese suzerainty means practical independence, whilst British suzerainty would entail subjection. It is not improbable that recent proceedings in Sikkim may have created doubts in the mind of the Chinese Resident at Lhassa whether some attempt might not be made to interfere with Nepal's allegiance to China, and hence the deputation to Khatmandu. The Chinese officers would only learn that the Government of India has scrupulously respected the independence of Nepal, and declined to interfere in local politics, even going the length of overlooking certain objectionable incidents in recognising the present administration. We are a little surprised that the *Mirror* should seem to suggest interference from Calcutta in the domestic affairs of Nepal, seeing that such interference could only be rendered effective by establishing complete political ascendancy, and we have always supposed the *Mirror* deprecated the assumption of additional responsibilities by the Government of India. Nepal is not at present, and is not likely to become in any sense, a menace to India; and while our political relations with the State continue satisfactory, there is no ground for interference in its domestic affairs of sufficient importance to render it worth while incurring the resentment, both in Nepal itself and on the part of China, which such interference would be certain to arouse. The Government of India may disapprove of the methods by which power is won and maintained in Nepal, and would possibly be pleased to see the Jung Bahadur family reinstated in the position from which they have been driven by Bir Shumshere and his brothers. But it is a wise policy that dictates a neutral attitude. The *Mirror* says that 'with Russia knocking at the North-West gate of India, the political activity of China on our northern frontier certainly wears a most suspicious appearance'. But we scarcely suppose our contemporary desires to seriously suggest that there is any menace to India involved in the deputation of a party of Chinese military officers from Lhassa to Khatmandu, or would advise the adoption of measures, the practical effect of which would be to deny China's suzerainty over Nepal and substitute British supremacy. The Nepalese cherish their relationship with China, as already remarked, because it is an easy and convenient yoke, and especially because they regard it as their main protection against a more real subjection to the Government of India. So strong is the feeling that we doubt if the exiled Nepalese princes would venture to accept an offer of British aid to regain their lost position, if the condition were an exchange of fealty to China for protection (accompanied by dictation) from India.

II.

NEPAL AFFAIRS.

Indian Mirror, Oct. 22, 1889.

The *Indian Daily News*, commenting on a paragraph about Nepal affairs, which appeared in our issue of the 1st instant, observes :—

> We are a little surprised that the *Mirror* should seem to suggest interference from Calcutta in the domestic affairs in Nepal, seeing that such interference could only be rendered effective by establishing complete political ascendancy, and we have always supposed the *Mirror* deprecated the assumption of additional responsibilities by the Government of India. Nepal is not at present, and is not likely to become, in any sense a menace to India; and while our political relations with the State continue satisfactory, there is no ground for interference in its domestic affairs of sufficient importance to render it worth while incurring the resentment, both in Nepal itself and on the part of China, which such interference would be certain to arouse. The Government of India may disapprove of the methods by which power is won and maintained in Nepal, and would possibly be pleased to see the Jung Bahadur family reinstated in the position from which they have been driven by Bir Shumshere and his brothers. But it is a wise policy that dictates a neutral attitude.

We certainly do think that Nepal could do us a good deal of mischief by opening her mountain passes to hordes of wild Tartars from the north; and this is more than a possibility under the rule of an intriguer, who respects neither human nor divine law. It has long been the policy of successive British statesmen to support on the throne of Afghanistan only such rulers as are friendly and loyal to the British alliance, so that through them we might retain in our hands the key of the north-west gate of India; and few, we venture to think, will refuse to recognise either the necessity or the wisdom of that policy. In the same way, it is to our interest, we think, that there should be a friendly Government in Nepal, on whose fidelity we could rely in barring our northern frontier against any possible irruption of the Central Asian hive. It is because we completely distrust Bir Shumshere as a most unscrupulous chicaner that we regard his coquetry with China with grave suspicion. Our contemporary, we are sure, cannot possibly have forgotten the incidents which led to our war with Nepal in 1814. The Gurkha State then disturbed the peace of British India under the influence of evil counsels; and it is not unlikely that the same thing might happen again with unprincipled men like Bir Shumshere at the helm of affairs in that State. Just as a dacoit or a Thug constitutes a source of danger to society, so a State, governed by turbulent and violent counsels, constitutes a menace to its neighbours: we measure alike the obnoxious character of both, not by the actual mischief they have done, but by their potentialities for evil. Hence the statesmanship that concerns itself only with the present, and does not take cognizance of the possibilities of the future, scarcely deserves the name. Our contemporary seems to think that the Government of India would be possibly pleased with the restoration of Jung Bahadur's family to power; but its recent policy in connection with Nepal is hardly calculated to favour such a belief. Was its precipitate recognition of Bir Shumshere a proof of its friendliness to that family? Was its contemptuous rejection of their appeals for assistance a proof of its sympathy for them? Does Mr. Veasey's notorious circular, said to have been issued to counteract the evil effect of their presence in India, or the irritating police espionage to which, we understand, they have been subjected, prove our overflowing good-will towards the exiled Nepalese princes? When the *Daily News* speaks of our satisfactory relations with Nepal, it seems to forget what really constitutes a State; it seems to forget that Bir Shumshere and his brothers alone do not constitute the kingdom of Nepal. Their interest in the country is precisely the interest of political adventurers, who would stick at nothing for the sake of power, and who, indeed, if the occasion arose, would not scruple to convert India's necessity into their personal opportunity.

It is our firm conviction that Bir Shumshere is playing a deep game in trying to establish a close connection with China. We are, therefore, inclined to think that so long as he is in power, there will be an element of danger to the Empire, for the existence of which Lord Dufferin's Government is to be held primarily responsible. His Lordship's advisers lamentably failed to take a statesman-like view of the situation in Nepal about three years ago, and the consequence was the adoption of a *laissez faire* policy, when it was our plain duty to face the position in a manly and generous spirit. The families of Jung Bahadur and Ranadip Sing have special claims to our consideration by reason of the services which the two brothers rendered to us in the past; and, under the existing treaty, we might have, to the mutual advantage of both States, assisted their families in recovering the position from which the latter have been ousted by the usurper. And this assistance we might have rendered them without in any way denying the suzerainty of China over Nepal, or making it a condition of such assistance that British political supremacy should be acknowledged by the Nepalese. It is the pride and glory of England that she is strictly faithful to her treaty engagements; and whether it be Prussia or Spain or Turkey, she has lavishly shed her blood and treasure in supporting her allies in Europe. But what an un-English spirit marks the recent policy of the Government of India in reference to Nepal! It has cast down constitutionalism, and set up revolution and anarchy as objects of political regard. It recognised Bir Shumshere with a most indecent haste; it overlooked, to the astonishment of all India, an attempt said to have been made on the life of its representative at Khatmandu at the instance of the usurper; nay, it went even further—it gave the latter a royal reception when he visited Calcutta in 1888, and removed with disgrace its old and trusted representative from Khatmandu because he was true and honest enough to lift his voice against the favourite of the hour, and to avow his sympathy for the exiled Princes. . . . .

Meanwhile, we would draw the particular attention of the Indian Political Agency in England to these facts. We are not a little surprised that they should have been so long overlooked by our English friends. The ungenerous treatment of Nepal and of the exiled Nepalese Princes by our Foreign Office, is a subject which ought to engage the serious attention of every Englishman interested in the maintenance of British rule in India on principles of justice and righteousness; and we would appeal to Mr. Bradlaugh, and to our other sympathising friends in Parliament, to earnestly take up this case with the view of ensuring a reversal of the unwise policy which the Government of India, under a gross misconception of the situation in Nepal, has been pursuing towards that unhappy State.